D1168377

CAN WE TRUST THE BIBLE?

CAN WE TRUST THE BIBLE?

Earl D. Radmacher
EDITOR

Tyndale House
Publishers, Inc.
Wheaton, Illinois

Library of Congress
Catalog Card Number
79-53863
ISBN 0-8423-4177-3, cloth
ISBN 0-8423-0207-7, paper

First printing,
September 1979
Printed in the
United States of America

To Him who said,
"Until heaven and earth pass away,
not the smallest letter or stroke
shall pass away from the Law,
until all is accomplished."

Matthew 5:18

CONTENTS

PREFACE

A story is told about telegraphers in the early days when they did not spell out punctuation in the process of transcribing a message. It seems that a wealthy lady on vacation in Europe wired her husband asking permission to purchase a very expensive item. The husband wired back, "No. Expense too great."

Without punctuation, the message read, "No expense too great." The lady bought the item, to the dismay of both husband and telegraph company. From then on, telegraphers spelled out punctuation—on all telegraph messages. This story illustrates how strategic and important details may be. Very little things can mean a lot.

This principle of the importance of factual detail is very germane to the current discussion among evangelicals about the inspiration and consequent authority of the Holy Scriptures. There are those who believe that you can have an authoritative Scripture without insisting that it be without error in factual data in areas such as history or science. On the other hand, there are those who insist that a doctrine of inspiration without inerrancy of the autographs (original writings) ultimately and logically results in Scriptures without final and absolute authority. Dr. James A. Borror has well stated the logic:

To the extent that you weaken inerrancy, to that extent you weaken inspiration. To the extent that you weaken inspiration, to that extent you have a garbled revelation. To the extent that you have a garbled revelation, to that extent you have a weakened authority. And when you weaken the authority of the Bible you launch upon a shifting sea of subjective uncertainty. ("Does it matter if the Bible makes mistakes?" The Standard, March 8, 1971, p. 21.)

A deep and growing concern over the strategic importance of the inerrancy of the autographs brought into existence, in 1977, The International Council on Biblical Inerrancy, which has as its purpose the defense and application of the doctrine of biblical inerrancy as an essential element for the authority of Scripture and a necessity for the health of the church. To make such an issue of inerrancy will bring the charge of "divisiveness" from some and "making mountains out of molehills" from others but, in the words of ICBI president James Montgomery Boice,

Members of the Council believe that they are simply calling a mountain a mountain and think it reasonable to expect that the ICBI will be a unifying force within evangelicalism, as it encourages Christian brothers and sisters to stand for the only objective foundation of a sure revelation from God there is—inerrancy.

The foregoing statement is taken from the preface of the first volume of the ICBI, namely, *The Foundation of Biblical Authority*, edited by Boice and containing six foundational position papers on inerrancy. The present volume is the second to come from the ICBI and contains the six stirring sermons that were preached in the plenary sessions of the Summit Conference at Chicago's Hyatt Regency in October of 1978. For those who were present, a common refrain after each of the plenary presentations was, "What a powerful proclamation! He was at his best!"

It is the prayer of the ICBI that as those messages of October 1978 are now presented in printed form, the Spirit of God shall so move upon you, the reader, that you will exclaim with us, "What the Bible says, God says—through human agents and without error." And may it not stop with exclamation but carry through in presentation "that you may prove yourselves to be blameless and innocent, children of God above reproach in the midst of a crooked and perverse generation, among whom you appear as light in the world, holding fast the word of life . . ." (Phil. 2:15, 16a).

Earl D. Radmacher, President
Western Conservative Baptist Seminary
Portland, Oregon

JAMES I. PACKER is Professor of Historical and Systematic Theology at Regent College, Vancouver, B. C. He was educated at Oxford University and is author of *"Fundamentalism" and the Word of God; Evangelism and the Sovereignty of God; God Speaks to Man; Knowing God;* and *I Want to Be a Christian.*

A LAMP IN A DARK PLACE
2 PETER 1:19–21
JAMES I. PACKER

My text is in 2 Peter, chapter one, verses 19–21. The apostle writes: "We have the word of the prophets made more certain, and you will do well to pay attention to it, as to a light shining in a dark place, until the day dawns and the morning star rises in your hearts. Above all, you must understand that no prophecy of Scripture came about by the prophet's own interpretation. For prophecy never had its origin in the will of man, but men spoke from God as they were carried along by the Holy Spirit."

I feel it is a great privilege and also a great responsibility to seek to interpret Scripture. If, like myself, you have inspected the redwoods in northern California, you have noticed that in the redwood preserves the trees are carefully fenced off. Perhaps you wondered why. The answer is that though they are enormous, they have a very shallow root system. And the constant tramp of visitors' feet can so loosen their roots as to make them very vulnerable to any wind that blows. That is why the fences are put up: to keep the

Bible quotations are from the *New International Version*

visitors from coming too near to them just in case they become too unstable and go over.

That says something to me. For a third of a century now, I have been a Christian, an evangelical Christian, watching evangelicalism. And I have come to think that in many ways, evangelicalism today is like the redwoods. I have seen marvelous growth in the Church of England, my own church, today. Something like a quarter of ministers in local churches have a definite evangelical commitment. That's utterly different from how it was thirty years ago. Here in the U.S.A. something like a fifth of the total population professes to be born again. That, I am sure, too, is a new thing. I've seen Christian literature prosper and expand, increase in quantity and deepen in quality, both at popular and specialists' levels. There was nothing like present-day Christianity in literature when my Christian pilgrimage began. I've seen great movements of evangelism. I've seen exciting movements of church renewal. I've lived through the period of the great congresses at Berlin and more recently at Lausanne. There has been great and wonderful growth.

But also it seems to me there has been an unmistakable shallowness. And as the years have gone by and the growth has increased, it seems to me that the shallowness, if anything, has become shallower, rather than being eliminated as the growth went on.

You say, "What do you mean?" I mean this: I am sure I have seen over this past generation a real weakening in doctrinal concern, in favor of an almost exclusive concentration on experience. If you feel right and you act zealous, well, doctrine doesn't matter. I have seen uncertainty and confusion in all sorts of surprising places with regard to quite basic beliefs; and in particular, with regard to the nature and use of the Bible, which is the source of all our beliefs. Of course, when there is uncertainty here, well, you can only expect to find uncertainty everywhere else. I have seen in my time churches and teaching institutions slip away from the Bible. And I have been troubled.

I believe that the work that we are doing and the work which is planned at this summit could, under God, do much for the roots of evangelicalism in our time. The alternative I fear to some effective concern for the roots is that we get shallower and shallower. And what will the outcome of that be? Soon I fear we may get swept away. I am sorry to start on such a gloomy note, but this is how I see it.

I believe a statement on inerrancy is a most strategic thing that we have taken in hand in seeking to get foundations clear for the authority of the Word of God in the lives of Christians and of the Christian church. We've got to go deep, if we are going to touch the heart of the biblical problem in our time.

Maybe you've heard the story of the doctor that was called in to a patient with acute abdominal pains, and straightaway he gave him a pill, and a person looking after him said, "Oh, doctor, is that going to make him better?" And the doctor said, "No, but it's going to give him a fit and I can cure fits." God forbid that we should ever handle the real needs of the church in our time like that.

Look at these words of our text. They are words of the Apostle Peter, the anchor man of the early church. They are words from the second letter that he wrote, using, I think, a different *amanuensis* to compose it for him from Silvanus, the man whose help he employed in the first letter. And that explains why the style of 2 Peter is different from the style of the first letter, and why the difference has nothing whatever to do with doubts about authorship. It's Peter writing, as he believes, his very last words of testimony and instruction to those who have been the recipients of his ministry, those for whom he has recognized pastoral responsibilities, those to whom he has sought to minister the things of God over the years.

He knows that his death is near. He speaks of it in 1:14. "I know," he says, "that I will soon put it aside [the tent of this body], as our Lord Jesus Christ has made clear to me." And so he writes the second letter to remind them of things that he has taught them already and to confirm them in those things. He says again, in verse 12, "I will always remind you of these things, even though you know them and are firmly established in the truth you now have." And again verse 15: "I will make every effort to see that after my departure you will always be able to remember these things."

And you say, "What are these things?" The answer is clear. They are the things concerning the knowledge of Jesus Christ the Lord. "Jesus Christ our Lord and Savior," as Peter says in verse 2. And again in verse 3, and again in verse 8 of this chapter. It's a favorite phrase of this letter and it comes again in the very last words that Peter speaks, in 3:18, where he summons his readers to "grow in the grace and knowledge of our Lord and Savior Jesus Christ." This has been the burden of Peter's ministry all along, and it's these things concerning Jesus Christ the Savior and Lord that he wants to enforce in this last letter.

And here in the section from which our text comes, he is dwelling on the power and coming of our Lord Jesus Christ. You have that phrase in verse 16. In verse 3 Peter spoke of the power of Christ, whereby he gives life—how his power has given us everything we need for life and godliness. And the coming of our Lord Jesus Christ, that great climactic event of human history, in the light of which all of God's people must live and look forward to every day of their life. And in verses 16–18, speaking of these things, he has been confirming the reality, the truth, the reliability of the things he has taught them concerning Jesus Christ, God's Son, by referring to the transfiguration, that great event of which he himself was an eyewitness.

"We did not follow cleverly invented stories," he says in verse 16. (Incidentally, that word for stories is "myths" and that word "myths" in the first century, just as today, meant "a story which whatever its significance for you hasn't got a factual basis.") That is the point that Peter is making here. "We didn't follow cleverly invented myths." "We didn't stuff you up with stories that have no factual basis when we told you about the power and coming of our Lord Jesus Christ," he says. "No, we were eyewitnesses of his majesty. We saw and heard. He received honor and glory from God the Father; a voice came to him from the majestic glory saying, 'This is my Son, whom I love; with him I am well pleased.' We saw it, we heard it," says Peter. "Take it from me."

And then, amazingly, in verse 19 he goes on to say, "Don't just take it from me. And don't even *primarily* take it from me. We have a more sure source of knowledge about Christ, even than the eyewitness testimony; we have something more firm, more sure, more reliable." He does say, you note, "We have," putting himself alongside them. "Something more sure from me," says Peter, "although I saw and heard. Something more sure for you, although I've been telling you what I saw and heard." Do you see what he is doing?

His thought is running in entirely the opposite direction to the way that we so often commend the faith today. We say, "Yes, it's written in the Bible. Let me show you; let me turn to the text; read it with me. And more than that, it works. Let me tell you my experience and I'll show you how it works." And we move from Scripture to personal witness, to personal experience, as if that were the more sure thing. But Peter here is doing exactly the reverse. "Now," he says, "we have something more sure than any testimony that you can hear from me. We have the word of the prophets, which is more certain."

"The prophetic Word," he says, "is more sure even than my eyewitness as an apostle to what happened at the transfiguration." You say, "That's an amazing thing for Peter to say. Why should he speak of Scripture as 'more sure even than this'?" One way to understand this is apostolic modesty; are we to understand it perhaps even as apostolic uncertainty? No, it's not precisely that. Peter's point is rather different.

When he speaks of the word of the prophets, the prophetic Word, what he is thinking of is, as all the commentators agree, the Old Testament as a whole. All of it was regarded as prophetic. Moses was a prophet and the historians were thought of as prophets, the former prophets, and all the teachers and spokesmen for God in the Old Testament were prophets too, as those first century men understood the matter. And the nature of the prophetic Word was that it was, in truth, God teaching, God preaching, God addressing men, God instructing men in the most direct way through, to be sure, the utterance of human agents. But the Word that they spoke was most directly and most categorically his Word and not their own. "Thus saith the Lord," they would say, and this was to alert all who heard them, and later all who read what they wrote, that what was now to be presented was not the private idea of Jeremiah, or Isaiah, or Ezekiel, or whomever, but it was the Word of the Lord God himself, speaking directly through his prophetic spokesman.

And the point Peter is making is this: "God has spoken in their prophetic Word. And what I say, and what the voice that I heard from heaven said, can only be right if it is in line with that prophetic Word." The prophetic Word confirms it. It is not the other way around. The prophetic Word confirms that Peter's experience is right, that the voice that he heard from heaven was indeed the voice of God. The Word is more sure, more certain, more reliable. The Word confirms all our experience now. That's the point that Peter is making. Take it ultimately, he says, from the Word.

And that suggests three matters about which I invite you to reflect with me a little now. First, the sureness of the Word. Three questions here. What does Peter's statement cover?

Well, it covers the whole of the Old Testament, for all the Old Testament was understood as prophetic in those days. Taking the total testimony of Peter's letter, we are made to realize that it covered apostolic writings, too. For in 2 Peter 3:15, in a passage which by implication is exhorting all his readers to study of the Scriptures, Peter speaks of what our dear brother Paul also wrote with the wisdom that God gave him. "He writes the same way in all his letters," Peter continues. "Speaking in him of these matters, his letters contain some things that are hard to understand." Yes, we can agree with that. "Things which are hard to understand, which ignorant and unstable people distort, as they do the other Scripture, to their own destruction." Isn't that striking? Here in the Apostolic Age, Peter is already comparing the letters of his brother, Paul, with the other Scriptures, classifying them as Scripture themselves.

And really there is nothing unnatural in that. Peter knew what apostolic inspiration was. Peter, after all, enjoyed it himself. And Peter understood that apostolic inspiration under the New Testament corresponded to prophetic inspiration under the Old. The psychological mode might be different, but the effect—men seeking the heart of God in words which God himself gave them —was identical in both cases. So, we may take what Peter says about the prophetic Word, that sure Word, more sure than anything one sees or hears or experiences, indeed, the test of all that one experiences —we can apply that to the New Testament writings no less than to the Old.

Another question. Whence does the sureness derive? Here again the answer is clear. From the divine origin of this prophetic Word; from the fact that it is God's Word. It has, if you like, a dual authorship. The men are its secondary authors; God is its primary author. This is, of course, how Peter himself is spelling it out in verses 20, 21. "You must understand," says Peter, "[this is very important], that no prophecy of Scripture came about by the prophet's own interpretation of things." This wasn't his own private idea; nothing of the kind.

"Prophecy never had its origin in the will of man, but men spoke from God as they were carried along by the Holy Spirit"—carried along in the way that a ship is carried along by the wind. The Greek word used would be used for a ship with the wind in its sails. Scripture is more sure than any other source of knowledge, just because it is directly and essentially, the testimony, Word, or witness of God. When you have Jeremiah receiving God's promise in the first chapter of his book, "I have put my words in your mouth," Jeremiah is being told what divine inspiration means.

In Acts 4:25, the story of the first recorded Christian prayer meeting, you have the early church praying, "Sovereign Lord, . . . You spoke by the Holy Spirit through the mouth of your servant, our father David: 'Why do the nations rage, and the people plot in vain?' " In Acts 28:25 you have Paul saying to the Jews in Rome, "The Holy Spirit spoke the truth . . . through Isaiah the prophet." You have New Testament Christians acknowledging that God put his Word in the mouth of these Old Testament men. You have the writer to the Hebrews quoting Scripture as he does, as the Word directly of the Father and the Son and the

Holy Spirit. And you have our Lord Jesus himself saying in Mark 12:36: "David himself, speaking by the Holy Spirit, declared, 'The Lord said to my Lord: Sit at my right hand until I put your enemies under your feet.'" When you have those words spoken in the New Testament record, you have witness being borne that the nature of Old Testament Scriptures is in truth God's words in men's mouths.

This view of the nature of the Scriptures, please note, is not the instrumental view of inspiration which is so popular today: the view that Scripture is essentially human witness first and foremost; human witness to God and his grace. Human witness, God-aided, of course, but human witness to the gospel of Christ in and through which God now speaks to men's hearts. This view allows you to discount details of what the biblical witnesses say. That is not the view that Peter is putting forward. He doesn't start with the humanity. He starts with the divinity. And his view of the nature of Scripture is not simply instrumental, human witness which God uses; rather his view of the nature of Scripture can be called incarnational. For to Peter the words of Scripture are simply the human form, the human nature, we might say, of God's own witness.

Peter starts with the testifying God. And he says the reason why God speaks through these biblical writings to us now is because he spoke through them once for all, when he gave them. They are the means of God's Word to us now, the most sure source of spiritual knowledge that we have. The view which we must take of inspiration, according to Peter, is an incarnational view in this sense: that just as in the Person of Jesus Christ you see the Son of God having taken to himself human nature, that his essential identity is his divine identity; so in the Scriptures we see the human form which God's Word took to itself, but its essential identity is that it is God's Word.

Men spoke from God, being borne along by the Holy Spirit. Their (the men's) word is the Word of God, because of its divine origin. It is so before ever God uses it to communicate to us today. And because it is God's own Word, it is universal in its relevance, even though it is particular in its form. The Bible is a set of particular writings from the ancient world—that is, putting the matter humanly—just as Jesus Christ is a particular Jew of the first century, A.D. But just as Jesus Christ is God's Son for the world, so Holy Scripture is God's Word for the world. In the particular, there, is the universality of God. Because the Bible is the Word of God, it is utterly trustworthy and utterly authoritative for our lives—not just relatively so, as being the best source we have, but absolutely so, as being God's pure word of address which stands for all eternity.

All right, this is the source as Peter understands the matter from which the sureness of the sure Word comes: in its testimony to Christ, and in its testimony to all things otherwise derived. My third question is: "What is all this saying to us, here and now?"

I believe it comes to us as a word of positive and definite encouragement, telling us that we are right to be here and right to be seeking to do together the thing that we are doing. Our concern revolves around the word "inerrancy." We are saying that the authority of Scripture lacks substance unless the inerrancy of Scripture is affirmed as its basis. Some folk today question whether the word "inerrancy" is helpful. I value it and I would like to tell you why.

It is in truth, in the scriptural sense of the word a "Shibboleth"; that is to say, a touchstone whereby things are known. I know that word Shibboleth has bad vibrations and has been cheapened today, but you remember how that word originally came to be used. In Judges 12 we read how the Gileadites and Jephthah possessed themselves of the fords of the River Jordan, and when an Ephraimite, one of their enemies, came across, they would ask him if he was an Ephraimite. Well, of course, he would say "No." But then they would ask him to say the word, "Shibboleth." And if he was an Ephraimite, he couldn't say it, and then they knew who he really was, and they dealt with him accordingly.

The word "Shibboleth," which Ephraimites couldn't pronounce, was a touchstone of their identity, and told the Gileadites who and what they really were. Now I want to put it to you, that this word inerrancy is similarly a touchstone of what people really mean when they speak of the authority of the Bible. If inerrancy is denied, as it tends to be by those of our friends who think of the inspiration of Scripture in instrumental terms only, then that which has authority for them is only an edited Scripture, a Scripture minus those bits and pieces which they think are wrong. And of course, there is no higher court of appeal for them than what they think; and what they think today, they may change their mind about tomorrow. And it has to be said by their friends, for their friends see it more clearly, I think, than they themselves, that once you start along this line, all certainty is gone. This too I have seen before.

I come to this conference from the Church of England. And in the Church of England in the first decade of this century, there was a group of folk brought up in the good, old evangelical way who began to call themselves Liberal Evangelicals because, they said, "We can allow ourselves to doubt the total truth of Scripture and the biblical view of the atonement, the death of Christ, and we shall not lose anything of the vitality of evangelical faith, but we shall be able to make adjustment to modern theology, and that will give us greater influence in the country." Two generations have passed. Those who were the pioneer Liberal Evangelicals were, in fact, brought up in old paths and had the root of the matter in them. In the 1940s, when spiritually I began to sit up and take notice, the Liberal Evangelicals appeared to be carrying everything before them and Evangelicals of the older type were a very small minority in the Church of England, with a very poor public image.

In the 1970s however, another generation has gone by, and the situation is reversed. The children and the grandchildren of the first Liberal Evangelicals have now ceased to call themselves Evangelical in any form at all. Most of them are in the radical camp. I mean the camp (for this word radical has quite a precise meaning in England) of those who doubt the deity of Jesus and doubt the resurrection of Jesus and call in question the Trinity and do not expect the personal return of Jesus and have no doctrine of the atonement. They understand new birth not in terms of entering into a new life but simply of turning over a new leaf. Naturalism has come in and swallowed them up. That's the way it goes. And when I hear my brother, Francis Schaeffer, asking apropos of the weakened view of biblical authority and biblical inspiration that's going the rounds today, "What is this going to do for our grandchildren?" I say, "Brother, you are asking the right question!" My English experience enables me to answer it. I know what it will do for our grandchildren, if in fact it isn't scotched.

Peter affirms ontological inspiration—inspiration comparable to the incarnation of Christ himself. He is the Son of God; the Bible is the Word of God. Therefore, Peter affirms that the whole of Scripture is authoritative, and its authority is the authority of God. Now he says, and surely we can begin to see something of the weight of what he is saying now, "We have the word of the prophets made more certain, and you will do well to pay attention to it, as to a light shining in a dark place."

I think I know why some of my brethren have abandoned biblical inerrancy. Partly they have been offended by unhappy things which believers in biblical inerrancy have sometimes done in interpreting the Bible, and partly they have been bothered by those minor discrepancies of detail which still are with us, though, may I say, not the same ones that were with our fathers and our grandfathers. The law of the study of discrepancies seems to be that one generation's problems come to be solved in the next generation and a fresh crop of little problems emerge for that generation to pass on to the next generation and so it goes. But there are these little discrepancies and it seems to be part of the discipline of the life of faith that we should be living with them and acknowledging that because the Bible is the Word of God, these things must be optical illusions. If we can't see it now, we may believe it, and maybe our children will see it to be so as knowledge increases, just as we in our day have seen the removal of these little problems which bothered our fathers.

On this matter of discrepancies I remember something which I read in an old seventeenth-century Puritan named William Bridge, a rather sweet passage in which he says that harping on discrepancies shows a very bad heart. "For the Godly man," he says, "it should be as it was with Moses." Then he appeals to Exodus 2. "When a Godly man sees the Bible and secular data apparently at odds, well, he does as Moses did when he saw an Egyptian fighting an Israelite, he kills the Egyptian. He discounts the secular testimony, knowing God's Word to be true." But, says Bridge, "When he sees an apparent inconsistency between two passages of Scripture, he does as Moses did when he found two Israelites quarreling. He tries to reconcile them. He says, 'Aha, these are brethren. I must make peace between them.' And that's what the Godly man does," says William Bridge. It's quaint, but it's rather sweet, and I think very true. A word from three hundred years ago for us.

But, as I say, though I understand how it is that some of my brethren have abandoned inerrancy in these days, I think it a tragic weakening of their witness. I think it means that the Bible, which they profess to acknowledge as authority, becomes a nose of wax for them. They can bend it any way they like; there is no certainty for them about what it says. But Peter's words can only encourage us to go on seeking to bear our witness in line with his witness to the divinity of God's Word written.

There is another matter on which I invite you to meditate with me also—a word about the darkness of the dark place. "You do well to pay attention to the Scripture, the prophetic Word, the Word which men spoke from God, as they were carried along by the Holy Spirit. For," says Peter, "it's as a light shining in a dark place." That word "dark" is one which you use in Greek for a dingy place, like a cellar, cow shed, or mine. And you can see, straightway, the thought that Peter is picking up here. It's a thought parallel to that which you've got in Psalm 119:105, that well-known verse where the psalmist says, "Your word is a lamp to my feet and a light for my path." By its light I can see to go. Without its light I could never see to go.

That's the point that he is making here. It's a picture. Here he is and it's dark and he's got a journey to take, and in the dark he can't see the path. The country is rough and if he tries to travel in the dark, he'll slip and stumble and fall, and he'll hurt himself. Someone kindly gives him a light. And you know what happens when you've got a light. You hold it up in front of you, your torch, your lamp, whatever it is; it isn't the same as the sun coming up. It doesn't banish all the darkness, but it does banish that little bit of darkness in front of you so that you can see to go. That's what your torch is for.

Well, that, I believe, is Peter's thought here. You do well to pay attention to the Word, he says, as "to a light shining in a dark, dingy place." A place, I think, which is indoors rather than out, though the Greek word doesn't make that absolutely certain. A place which maybe is actually dirty. This may be, as part of the murk and the dirt needs to be shown up so that it can be removed. But a place, certainly, where there are many obstacles which you need the light in order to avoid. You know what it's like trying to make your way through a furnished room in total darkness. You don't know where the furniture is—you trip over it; you bang your legs; you can hurt yourself quite considerably by running into things. You need a light, and, says Peter, "you do well to pay attention to God's Word. God's Word written is as a light that shines in a dark place to enable you to avoid the obstacles and see your way and maybe clean it up and remove the dirt."

Why does he speak of the place where we are as dark? Well, because that's how the world is. It is a world of moral laxity. We haven't time to glance at chapter two of this letter in which Peter pinpoints some of the moral laxity, the permissiveness that was running not only in the world but in the church in his day, but I invite you to read it at your leisure and tremble. It's pretty grisly. And as you know, we have this kind of thing today.

Three nights ago I was in a student meeting. A young man said to me afterwards, "I was talking to a friend of mine last week and I didn't know what to say to him. He was urging that it's perfectly all right to be a minister and a practicing homosexual. What was I to say to him?" The man had never thought that he would be asked such a question. He had been completely dumbfounded by hearing it. I said, "Well, would he think it right to be a minister if he were a practicing fornicator?" I went on with him along that line, which I think is the scriptural line to take. But these things, we know, are being said in the church. And indeed, there are some who are acting on these principles. It's a dark world. It's a dark church. It's bewildering. We need light. Thank God, we have in the written Word the light that we need.

If anyone should say to us, "Is it you, you troubler of Israel, stirring up dust, forcing people to argue and debate about inerrancy?" we should have to reply, as Elijah replied when a similar thing was said to him, "It's not we that trouble Israel, but trouble comes with those who are leading Israel astray over the truth and authority of the Word of God." Who is putting out the light? And who is seeking to put on the light? I don't think I need to say any more on that point.

Bless God for the light that he has given us for our journey through this dark world. That light is, namely, the Holy Scriptures, the inspired Word which shines as a light in this very dark place. Learn to thank God for the Word and to commend what we believe about it, by the way in which we treasure it, read, mark, learn, and inwardly digest it. I remember a book of mine in which there was this precious misprint, "RSV*P* means Revised Standard Version," but RSVP is in truth what God has had written in the front of our Bibles for us all. The Word is for us to treasure up in our hearts and respond to in faith. God give us grace so to do, to say with Isaac Watts, "My hiding place, my refuge, tower, and shield art Thou, O Lord. I firmly anchor all my hope in thy unerring Word." Let this be the Word of our hearts as we attend to the light which God has given to us to shine in this dark place, and by God's grace we shall do well.

DR. EDMUND P. CLOWNEY is president and Professor of Practical Theology at Westminster Theological Seminary. He is a graduate of Wheaton College and Westminster Seminary, earned a graduate degree at Yale Divinity School, and did graduate study in missions at Union Theological Seminary, New York. He served Orthodox Presbyterian pastorates for ten years before joining the teaching staff at Westminster in 1952. He was the first "Eutychus" in *Christianity Today,* and is the author of *Eutychus and His Kin, Preaching and Biblical Theology, Called to the Ministry, The Doctrine of the Church,* and *Christian Meditation.*

HOW CHRIST INTERPRETS THE SCRIPTURES
LUKE 24:26, 27
EDMUND P. CLOWNEY

What authority does the Bible have? How are we to interpret what the Bible says? These two questions trouble many Christians today. Some are ready to scale down the authority of the Bible. It is, after all, a human book, they say. It was written long ago, and we cannot be bound by what it says about marriage, or about other religions, or even about God. Others would claim to acknowledge the authority of the Bible as God's Word but they offer new ways of interpreting the Bible. They give new meaning to a Greek term, "hermeneutics" to describe a field of study that links contemporary philosophy with linguistics. One approach in hermeneutics has been called "demythologizing." It assumes that modern man can no longer credit the supernaturalism of the Bible. It therefore undertakes to assign a mythical value to Biblical accounts of such miracles as Christ's resurrection and his birth of the Virgin. These "myths" are then translated to yield religious meaning even though their historical value has been denied.

But before we make today's philosophy and the

Bible quotations, unless otherwise indicated, are from the *American Standard Version.*

assumptions of our own culture the standard for our interpretation of the Bible we need to inquire again about what the Bible says on this very issue of interpretation. There the tables are turned. God's Word summons us to stand before him and to question our own assumptions. This appears clearly in the account with which Luke concludes his gospel. There we hear the risen Christ interpreting the Scriptures, and we will do well to consider it.

Cleopas and a companion, two disciples of Jesus, were returning on the first Easter morning to their home in Emmaus, a village not far from Jerusalem. Jesus, alive from the dead, joined them, but they were kept from recognizing him. He asked the cause of their sorrowful conversation. They expressed surprise. Could it be that anyone leaving Jerusalem did not know of the crucifixion of Jesus? "We hoped," they said, "that it was he who should redeem Israel" (Luke 24:21). Jesus said, " 'O fools, and slow of heart to believe all that the prophets have spoken: Ought not Christ to have suffered these things, and to enter into his glory?' And beginning at Moses and all the prophets, he expounded unto them in all the scriptures the things concerning himself" (Luke 24:25–27, KJV).

Fools? Cleopas and his companion were stung by the Stranger's rebuke. They had thought that he was the one who was out of touch—uninformed about the recent events in Jerusalem. They were well-informed; as insiders, they knew the facts. But the facts they knew left them thoroughly confused. How could any clear picture emerge from the disaster of the crucifixion, and the unsettling rumors of the empty tomb? They had trusted in Jesus. Theirs was the attitude of faith. Surely what *could* be understood they understood. But the events were just too much for them.

Yet the Stranger called them *fools*. They knew the Scriptures but they did not understand them. They had witnessed the works and words of Jesus, but they had missed their meaning. They understood neither the Scriptures nor the Lord.

When the risen Christ met them he did not at once reveal himself to them. He did not cry, "Cleopas!" as at the garden tomb he had cried, "Mary!" Rather, he taught them what they should have known, expounding from the Old Testament the necessity of the sufferings of the Christ and the glory to follow. Their eyes were not to be opened to know the Lord until their minds were opened to know the Scriptures. After all, even an appearance on the road to Emmaus might be like the women's vision of angels: only another in a series of disturbing phenomena. Fools could cling to such confusion. But men whose hearts burned with the prophet's vision of Christ, men who saw the Lord in the Word, such men were prepared to see him in the flesh of his resurrection. Indeed, such men could believe even though they did not see him. They need not with their own eyes watch him break bread with Cleopas or reach out his scarred hand to Thomas. In teaching Cleopas, Christ was teaching us, for we too are often fools and slow of heart to believe. The naive savants of our day take it for granted that they are the first to have access to the full confusion of the facts. The study of the history of religions, we are told, has now shown us the weird ancient world of the Old Testament. We can now reconstruct the social and religious settings of particular texts and trace much of the complex development of tradition, oral and written, by which these texts were handed down.

With all this learning stacked about us it is assumed that we cannot possibly adopt the teaching of the New Testament about the Old. Claims of fulfilled prophecy are dismissed with contempt or set aside more gently as interpretations fitting the times in which they were made. Indeed, much current Biblical scholarship sees itself as a bold salvage operation seeking the means to preserve something analogous to Biblical convictions in the totally different world of the modern mind.

If for no other reason, we are told, we cannot accept the New Testament's citations of the Old because they are taken out of context. We cannot return, it is said, to an unhistorical view of Scripture that hears each text as a mysterious oracle, pregnant with a meaning that is not in the least evident in its original setting.

Such an estimate of the teaching of the apostles reflects, of course, on the teaching of Jesus in this passage. Surely Luke is not reporting here words of Jesus that were lost with the Ascension. The exposition of the Old Testament that Jesus began on the road to Emmaus was continued during his ministry on earth in the forty days after the resurrection. That teaching provided the framework for the preaching and teaching of the apostles as reported in Acts and the rest of the New Testament.

Our own preaching and teaching of Christ must follow the apostolic model presented by Jesus himself. When we seek to renew our understanding in this pattern we are often warned that this is fundamentalist folly. The contemporary masters of interpretation tell us that we cannot go back to Emmaus to renew our hermeneutics. But Jesus was dismayed by a different folly. How can men be so slow of heart to believe all that the prophets have spoken?

According to Jesus, Messianic prophecy is a theme that fills the Old Testament in every part—the law of Moses, the prophets, the psalms—these are the major divisions of the Old Testament Scriptures. It is a pervasive theme, found in all the prophets. As Peter says, "Yea, and all the prophets from Samuel and them that followed after, as many as have spoken, they also told of these days" (Acts 3:24).

It is a theme that has a pattern: that Christ must

suffer these things and enter into his glory.

Is there a believing understanding of the Old Testament open to us? Can we enter into that grasp of the Scriptures that seemed so self-evident to Jesus Christ? In particular, can we really discern the pattern of suffering and glory of which Jesus speaks?

On the road to Emmaus Jesus interprets the Scriptures in their focus and pattern. In their focus, for he shows the authority of Scripture as the Word of the Lord and how Scripture focuses on the Lord of the Word. In their pattern, too, for Jesus discloses the theme of his sufferings and glory of which all the Scriptures speak.

Jesus' amazement at the folly of those disciples leaving Jerusalem on Easter morning reflects indeed the reality of his own experience of resurrection life. Jesus knew the explosion of life, joy, and glory that lifted him from the tomb. How could these disciples perceive it as a curious rumor purveyed by a few women—only a few and, of course, only women?

But Christ's amazement also takes account of the information those disciples had. The angels at the tomb had reminded the women of Jesus' teaching. Jesus had predicted not only his arrest, delivery to the Romans, and crucifixion. He had also promised his resurrection on the third day (Luke 18:33). Yet Jesus does not simply appeal to his former teaching. Rather he appeals to Scripture, for it was in Scripture that his teaching was grounded. "It was necessary" for the Christ to suffer these things and to enter into his glory. The necessity is the necessity of fulfilling the Scriptures.

So Jesus taught through all his ministry. He taught with an authority that astonished his hearers (Luke 4:32), but his authority confirmed the Scriptures of the Old Testament. Indeed, just where Jesus most sharply contrasts the new with the old, just where he proclaims the new wine of the kingdom and the fire of the Spirit that his coming brings, just there Jesus most clearly shows that the new is the fulfillment of the old. The fire of the Spirit is the promise of the Father (Luke 3:16; 24:49). "The law and the prophets were until John; from that time the gospel of the kingdom of God is preached" (Luke 16:16). Are the law and the prophets then set aside? No, they are fulfilled, for "it is easier for heaven and earth to pass away, than for one tittle of the law to fall" (Luke 16:17).

Jesus' parable of the rich man and Lazarus anticipates his Scripture lesson on the road to Emmaus. The rich man in torment would have Lazarus sent back from the dead to warn his brothers of the consequences of their luxurious life-style. Abraham replies, "If they hear not Moses and the prophets, neither will they be persuaded, if one rise from the dead" (Luke 16:31). Apart from an understanding of the Old Testament, even Christ's resurrection will not bring conviction.

What Jesus asserted about Scripture is equally evident in what he taught from Scripture. He discerns the unfolding of the Father's plan in the incidents of Old Testament history. Elijah's ministry to the widow of Zarephath and Elisha's healing of Naaman the leper reveal God's great purpose of bringing mercy to the Gentiles when Israel is judged for hardness of heart (Luke 4:25–27). In the Scriptures God reveals his own nature as well as his purpose. Jesus argues for the resurrection from the passage where God speaks to Moses from the burning bush (Luke 20:37). His argument appeals to Moses' own record of the words spoken to him by God. God revealed himself to Moses as the God of Abraham, Isaac, and Jacob. Jesus argues in an amazing way that the God who is known as the God of Abraham cannot be the God of Abraham's memory. Because God is the living God, those who are bound to him by the bonds of his grace must live unto him. That argument could hardly be less convincing from a humanistic perspective. Its power comes from the authority of Jesus' knowledge of God. The God who can be named by the name of Abraham is the living God, and therefore he cannot abandon Abraham to death and still be called by Abraham's name as the God of the Covenant.

Jesus' knowledge of his Father shown in that teaching is expressed also in his assurance about Scripture. The testimony of Moses comes with the authority of God's own Word. Therefore the issues of life and death may safely be inferred from it.

Not only does Jesus enforce the authority of God's Word in his teaching; he obeys that Word as the Lord's Anointed. When Jesus is driven by the Spirit into the desert after his baptism, he meets the temptations of the devil with the authority of the Word of God. Satan tempted Jesus specifically with reference to his messianic sonship. He would have Jesus use his powers to deliver himself from the ordeal of testing: "Turn these stones into bread!" Or he would offer Jesus the kingdoms of the world without the cross: "Do obeisance to me!" Or he would push Jesus to put God to the test: "Jump from the pinnacle of the temple!" In every temptation Jesus appeals to what is written, setting the authority of God's Word against the wiles of the devil. "It is written, Man shall not live by bread alone, but by every word that proceedeth out of the mouth of God" (Matt. 4:4; Luke 4:4).

Jesus taught from the Scriptures, pressing their claims upon his hearers; he obeyed the Scriptures, recognizing the claims of God's Word on his own ministry. But more, Jesus *fulfilled* the Scriptures, he claims the Scriptures as no other can, for he affirms that Moses and the prophets wrote of him. The authority of Scriptures cannot be separated from Jesus Christ. The Word of the Lord bears witness to the Lord of the Word. The salvation to which the prophets looked forward with such yearning is fulfilled in Christ; the Spirit of prophecy by which they spoke is the Spirit of Christ in them (1 Pet. 1:11).

The Scriptures find their source and their focus in Christ. Jesus Christ stood up to read the prophecy of Isaiah in the synagogue of Nazareth, "The Spirit of the Lord is upon me, because he anointed me to preach good tidings to the poor . . . to proclaim the acceptable year of the Lord" (Luke 4:18, 19). His exposition of the passage was simple: "Today hath this scripture been fulfilled in your ears" (Luke 4:21).

Christ's understanding of the Scripture shaped his ministry. He deliberately and consciously fulfilled Scripture. He stood up in that synagogue in his home-town knowing that his claim would be rejected but compelled to make it, for the Scripture must be fulfilled. Nor is it only a few isolated incidents in his ministry that are determined by Scripture: his preaching of the gospel, his miracles, his triumphal entry into Jerusalem, his crucifixion, and resurrection. No, these are the heart of his ministry; it is the *whole* of his ministry that is determined by Scripture.

And yet more—Jesus in fulfilling Scripture is not like an actor in a play, carefully following the script and staging the appropriate emotions. This would be *playing* the Scriptures but not *fulfilling* them. Rather, it is in the ministry of Jesus that the real meaning of prophecy at last appears. If Jesus understood his ministry in the light of Scripture, then Jesus also understood the Scripture in the light of his ministry.

But deeper still: Jesus does not merely *act* in fulfillment of Scripture. He *is* the fulfillment. We would be desperately more foolish than the Emmaus disciples if we supposed that Jesus' view of Scripture was incidental to his saving work—that he was just a child of his times in holding to the authority of Scripture. To the contrary, Jesus understood himself as the Servant-Son of Scripture, the Messiah and the Lord. Luke well reflects Jesus' own understanding when he speaks of him both as the Lord's Christ (Luke 2:26) and as Christ the Lord (Luke 2:11). If Jesus had held another view of Scripture his teaching would not stand and his claims could not have been made. If we lose the Lord's Word we lose the Lord.

But Jesus *did* know the Scripture as the Word of God. He was and is its source and center. Moreover, in his interpretation of Scripture he both expects and demands that we receive the Bible as he does.

Jesus not only taught that the Scriptures bore witness to him. He expected us to receive that witness. Cleopas and his companion are fools and slow of heart to believe. If we find Christ in all the Scriptures only by a clever *tour de force,* we fail to do what Jesus expected. Jesus did not find it difficult to relate the Scriptures to himself. His interpretation was an opening process. He opened the Scriptures and he opened their minds (Luke 24:32, 45). The Bible is clear in its focus on Christ. If we miss it, the obstacle is not in the Bible but in us.

In its centering on Christ we find the Scriptures unified as well as clear. Obviously the New Testament is all about Jesus Christ. Look at the opening verses of each of the Gospels and see how each begins with Jesus. Turn to the salutations of Paul's epistles and read the name of the Lord. Take the letter to the Philippians and count the number of times Paul speaks of Jesus. Yes, the whole New Testament is about Jesus Christ. Apostles and prophets filled with Christ's Spirit have written concerning him. But this is not less true of the Old Testament, and the New Testament shows us that this is the case.

Ah, but is not the Old Testament about Israel? Yes, and who is the true Israel at last, God's true servant Israel, in whom he will be glorified (Isaiah 49:3)? Is not the Old Testament about Moses, Elijah, and the prophets? Yes, and who is the prophet like unto Moses, the One who talks with them on the Mount of

Transfiguration about his "exodus," his death to be accomplished at Jerusalem? Moses and Elijah depart, but Jesus only remains. The voice from the cloud that had spoken to Moses and Elijah now says, "This is my Son, my chosen: hear ye him" (Luke 9:35).

Is not the Old Testament about the Lord, the Shepherd of Israel who will come again marching through the desert to redeem his people? (Isa. 40; Psa. 23; Ezek. 34:11). Yes, and Jesus is the Lord, hailed by the herald angels, worshiped by doubting Thomas, "My Lord and my God" (John 20:28). He is the good Shepherd who gives his life for the sheep (John 10).

Not only do the Scriptures focus on Christ. They also trace a pattern: the pattern of his sufferings and the glory to follow. Jesus' interpretation of the Scriptures after his resurrection made this pattern central for the preaching and teaching of the church. Paul reasoned from the Scriptures that Christ must suffer and rise again from the dead (Acts 17:3). His epistles again and again present this theme. Peter writes that the Spirit of Christ in the Old Testament prophets "testified beforehand the sufferings of Christ, and the glories that should follow" (1 Pet. 1:11).

The sufferings of Christ appear in the Old Testament in the figure of the suffering servant-son. God's servant is righteous, yet he endures undeserved affliction for the name of God. Job's sufferings were not the punishment for his sins, as his friends insisted in their counseling sessions. In a way that Job could not understand, they brought glory to God. They showed that Job's service to the Lord was from the heart and not for material reward. In the Psalms the Lord's anointed cries out under the persecution of his enemies. He is hated without a cause (Psa. 69:4). He flees to God for refuge and judgment under the false accusations of his enemies (Psa. 7). The hatred of his enemies comes precisely because he is God's servant: ". . . for thy sake I have borne reproach . . . the zeal of thy house hath eaten me up; and the reproaches of them that reproach thee are fallen upon me" (Psa. 69:7, 9).

The first verse of Psalm 22 became the cry of Jesus on the cross: "My God, my God, why hast thou forsaken me?" That cry of abandonment is the most intense form of a cry that echoes through the Psalms, the cry of the righteous servant of the Lord in the agony of his suffering. Psalm 22 has the form that is most frequent in the whole book of Psalms, the lament of the individual sufferer. As Jesus fulfills this Psalm he fulfills this theme in all of these Psalms. In him the mystery of suffering reaches its climax. He is the only truly righteous Servant, the only King who can claim total faithfulness to God. Yet God who has promised never to fail or forsake his people forsakes his Holy One on the cross. There God the Father and God the Son pay the price of redeeming sinners.

The divisions of Psalm 22 all find their fulfillment in Christ. The whole Psalm is his. He describes his enemies circling about him like wild oxen, bulls, dogs, and lions. Not only do his enemies laugh at him with mocking malice; behind their laughter is the hatred of hell, the rage of the principalities and powers, the hosts of Satan.

But Jesus continues to trust. He yet calls God his God, the faithful God of the covenant (Psa. 22:3–5), his own God from the womb of his mother (Psa. 22:9, 10). His cry for salvation is heard, "Save me from the lion's mouth" (Psa. 22:21). Jesus did cry for deliverance, and was heard. The Psalm of agony can end with a shout of victory and praise. Yet Jesus' victory was won as he accepted the Father's will and trusted, even in the darkness of abandonment.

In John's Gospel we read of the heaviness of Christ's heart as he drew near to Calvary. "Now is my soul troubled," he said, using the language of the Psalms (John 12:27; Psa. 42:11). Should he ask to be saved from the coming hour? That prayer surely appears in the Psalms. "What shall I say? Father save me from this hour? But for this cause came I unto this hour" (John 12:27).

No, he will not seek his own will but the will of the Father. "Father, glorify thy name" (John 12:28). God's voice from heaven responded, "I have both glorified it, and will glorify it again." Jesus taught his disciples to pray, "Hallowed be thy name," and Jesus hallowed his Father's name as he went to the cross. For Jesus is not only the righteous servant, obedient to the Father's will; he is also the representative servant, suffering for the people of God. God's name is glorified by Jesus the sin-bearer, for God so loved the world that he gave his only-begotten Son.

In the Psalms the righteous sufferer is a representative figure, not the average man-in-the-street, but the Lord's anointed, the one chosen and set apart, with the unction of God's Spirit. The figure of the Messianic King appears not only in Psalm 110 where his rule is described, but in Psalm 22 where his suffering is so vividly portrayed. Jesus is that King, David's greater Son.

Scholars have debated the meaning of the title, "Son of man," the designation that Jesus used most often for himself. Since Jesus spoke of the Son of man coming in the clouds of heaven (Matt. 26:64) it seems clear that he is alluding to the passage in Daniel 7:13. There one like to the Son of man comes with the clouds of heaven to the Ancient of Days and is given an eternal kingdom. The contrast is between the world empires arising like beasts out of the sea and the human form of the ruler of God's eternal kingdom. The title, "Son of man" surely reflects the glory and the heavenly rule given to Christ. Yet Jesus uses the title not only in reference to the glory of his second coming but also in reference to his sufferings and death. "The Son of man must suffer many things . . . and be killed, and the third day be raised up" (Luke 9:22). No doubt the contrast is deliberate; Jesus will not establish his kingdom after the manner of Gentile emperors, but through suffering and death. He is the true Man, the second Adam. As the Son of man he holds title to man's dominion over the earth, the dominion that is celebrated in Psalm 8. But in his ministry the words of that Psalm take on deeper significance. He is made a little lower than the angels, not merely in taking human nature, but for the suffering of death (Psa. 8:5; Heb. 2:7–9) that he might redeem the sons of Adam.

The servant figure in the Old Testament is not only royal. The priest, too, is a servant of God and is called to suffering. Aaron as well as Moses was assailed by rebellious Israel (Num. 20:2), and the priests and Levites ceremonially bore the iniquity of the people (Num. 18:23). Jesus Christ comes as one who is in all things made like his brethren "that he might become a merciful and faithful high priest" who is able to save to the uttermost them that come unto God by him (Heb. 2:17, 18; 4:15; 7:25).

The prophets of the Old Testament also suffered as servants of the Lord. Think of the persecution of Jeremiah, cast into the pit because he faithfully prophesied the word of the Lord. Even Jonah's suffering, disobedient as he was, could be used as a symbol of the suffering servant, for Jonah was willing to drown in the sea so long as he did not have to go to Nineveh and thereby bring hope and deliverance to the enemies of the people of God. Jonah thought it better that one man should die so that his nation would not perish. Nineveh was the enemy capital. From its gates the armies would march to destroy the northern kingdom of Israel. God's word threatened that in forty days Nineveh would be destroyed. Jonah assumed that if he perished Nineveh would hear no message from God and in forty days would be obliterated in judgment. Jonah sadly misconceived God's mercy, yet he was willing to give his life for his people. In spite of himself Jonah provided the sign that Jesus used to depict his death, burial and resurrection (Matt. 12:39–42).

The servant figure blends the images of the suffering king, the suffering priest, and the suffering prophet. This is the figure Isaiah uses with such power in the servant songs of his prophecy. At last the calling of the people of God will be fulfilled in God's true Servant. God says to his individual servant, "It is too light a thing that thou shouldest be my servant to raise up the tribes of Jacob, and to restore the preserved of Israel: I will also give thee for a light to the Gentiles, that thou mayest be my salvation unto the end of the earth" (Isa. 49:6). But the individual Servant who will restore the preserved of Israel is himself the true Israel: "Thou art my servant; Israel, in whom I will be glorified" (Isa. 49:3).

Here is the reason for the fluid way in which the Servant songs can move back and forth between national Israel and personal Israel as the servant of God. The servant foreseen by Isaiah is greater than king Cyrus (who is also made God's servant to restore Israel from captivity—Isa. 45:1–7). But unlike Cyrus, the Lord's true Servant will receive his dominion through suffering. Indeed, in his suffering he will be identified with his people, for "he hath borne our griefs and carried our sorrows . . . he was wounded for our transgressions, he was bruised for our iniquities; the chastisement of our peace was upon him; and with his stripes we are healed" (Isa. 53:4, 5).

The theme of the suffering Servant that rises to such amazing grandeur in Isaiah 53 is not a strange interlude there, but lies deep in Old Testament theology.

In Isaiah's servant songs we find the righteous and representative Sufferer seen also as a Sin-bearer. The suffering Servant of God becomes the Lamb of God, the sacrificial offering for sin. The New Testament guides us in perceiving that the symbolism of the sacrificial system points us to Jesus Christ, "the Lamb of God that taketh away the sin of the world" (John 1:29). The requirement that the lamb of sacrifice must be without blemish is seen as symbolizing the perfect sinlessness of Jesus Christ (1 Pet. 1:19; Heb. 9:11; 13:12; Ex. 12:5; Num. 28:3). Like the animal in the sin-offering, Jesus must bear the curse. He is the passover Lamb; his blood sprinkles the mercy-seat to seal the finished atonement of his sacrifice on the cross. The whole book of Hebrews deals not only with Christ's work as our Priest but also with his offering of himself as our Sacrifice.

In a striking passage in the Old Testament the figures of sacrifice and sonship are joined in God's command to Abraham to offer Isaac as a sacrifice (Gen. 22). Abraham obediently takes Isaac up Mount Moriah. In a moment of supreme pathos, Isaac says to his father, "Behold the fire and the wood: but where is the lamb for a burnt-offering?" (Gen. 22:7). We can sense the anguish as well as the faith in Abraham's heart as he replies, "God will provide himself the lamb for a burnt-offering, my son" (v. 8). Jehovah-Jireh: "The Lord will see to it" —that is the message of the gospel. God did provide the lamb for the sacrifice; not simply in the animal caught in the thicket that Abraham could offer in place of his son, but in God's final Substitute. God provided the Lamb when he sent his only begotten Son to the cross. The Lamb is God's Isaac. Not only did the Son pay the price of sacrifice; the Father paid the price when he gave his only begotten Son (John 3:16).

Finally, the suffering of Jesus Christ is presented in the Old Testament in the figure of the smitten Shepherd. With amazing drama God reveals himself at Massah-Meribah as the Shepherd who bears the smiting (Ex. 17:1–7).

There in the wilderness Israel rebelled against God,

accusing him of having led them out into the wilderness where they must die of thirst. They were ready to court-martial Moses and execute him by stoning. But Moses rightly protests: "Why are you bringing suit against me? Why are you putting God on trial?" (see Ex. 17:2). The people of God were demanding a court case, charging God with covenant-breaking. "Is the Lord among us or not?" they asked—implying that he was not.

Do you remember God's word to Moses? "Pass on before the people, and take with thee of the elders of Israel; and thy rod, wherewith thou smotest the river, take in thy hand, and go" (v. 5). God was saying, "If the people demand a covenant law-suit, they shall have one. Take the rod of judgment, symbolizing my justice, assemble the people for a formal hearing and bring the elders to witness the judgment." The word "Meribah" contains a Hebrew root that is always used in the Old Testament of a law-case, a legal controversy.

Then God says to Moses something that is never said elsewhere in the Old Testament. God says, "Behold, I will stand before thee there upon the rock in Horeb" (v. 6). God will stand before a man. God will stand in the prisoner's dock. He will stand before the upraised rod of Moses, as though he were a guilty prisoner, sentenced to bow down before the judge and receive the stripes of judgment (Deut. 17:8–11; 25:1–3).

Still more—incredibly, God says to Moses, "Thou shalt smite the rock!" The rock on which God stands is the symbol of God himself. God's name is the Rock (Deut. 32:4, 31). Moses raises his rod and strikes the Rock. The people have called for judgment, for the very stroke of death. God is not the covenant-breaker. He does not deserve to be smitten. The people are guilty. Yet in this symbol of sovereign grace God comes to stand in their place and to bear the smiting. From the rock there flows forth water for the deliverance of the people. John reminds us in his Gospel, that when the spear was thrust into the side of the Lord there flowed forth blood and water (John 19:34). "Rock of Ages, cleft for me, let me hide myself in thee."

God himself identifies with the suffering of his people. "In all their affliction he was afflicted" (Isa. 63:9). God bore with his people in the wilderness. God is the Shepherd of his people. A shepherd is identified with his sheep. He goes before them and sleeps in their midst. He is identified with them; he bears with them. The great mystery of the Old Testament is that God is not only the covenant Lord who makes his demands upon his people, but the great God of grace who gives himself to his people, who is smitten in their stead, and who comes for their redemption. For the great text of all the Scriptures is this: "Salvation is of the Lord" (Jonah 2:9).

Christ in his sufferings is portrayed in the Old Testament not only as the Servant, but also as the Lord. That brings us to see how the glory of Christ is anticipated in the Old Testament. Jesus Christ is prophesied both as the glorified Servant and as the glorious Lord.

The Psalm of the suffering Servant, Psalm 22, becomes the Psalm of the glorified Servant. The cry of abandonment at the beginning of the Psalm, *"Eli, eli lama sabachthani,"* becomes the cry of triumph in verse 22. The writer of Hebrews quotes that verse, ascribing it to Jesus Christ: "I will declare thy name unto my brethren, in the midst of the congregation will I sing thy praise" (Heb. 2:12).

God's suffering Servant is the Victor because God has decreed his triumph: "Sit thou at my right hand, until I make thine enemies thy footstool" (Psa. 110:1). It is God who raises him up: "When he cried unto him, he heard. Of thee cometh my praise in the great assembly" (Psa. 22:24, 25). "When thou shalt make his soul an offering for sin, he shall see his seed, he shall prolong his days, and the pleasure of the Lord shall prosper in his hand" (Isa. 53:10, KJV).

God exalts his Servant because he has suffered: "Therefore will I divide him a portion with the great, and he shall divide the spoil with the strong; because he poured out his soul unto death, and was numbered with the transgressors; yet he bare the sin of many, and made intercession for the transgressors" (Isa. 53:12).

God exalts his Servant by raising him from the dead. Peter preached on Pentecost the fulfillment of Psalm 16: "Thou wilt not leave my soul unto Hades, neither wilt thou give thy Holy One to see corruption" (Psa. 16:10; Acts 2:27). The literal translation of King Hezekiah's prayer is fulfilled in Jesus Christ, "Thou has loved my soul from the pit" (Isa. 38:17). The beloved of the Father is loved from the pit. The gates of hell cannot hold him captive. They are burst open and Jesus Christ rises in glory. He ascends to God's right hand in triumph. "Lift up your heads, O ye gates; even lift them up, ye everlasting doors; and the King of glory shall come in" (Psa. 24:9, KJV).

Christ's heavenly dominion is that of the King on the throne (Ps. 110:1–3), but also of the Priest in the sanctuary: "The Lord hath sworn, and will not repent, Thou art a priest forever after the order of Melchizedek" (Ps. 110:4, KJV). His is a royal priesthood; John sees him standing in the sanctuary clothed in sovereign majesty. Read Psalm 110 and then turn to Paul's description of Christ's glory at the end of Ephesians 1. See how Paul uses the language of the Psalm: Christ is made to sit at God's right hand (Eph. 1:20; Psa. 110:1), all things are in subjection under his feet (Eph. 1:22; Psa. 110:1), Christ's head is lifted up as he is made head over all things (Eph. 1:22, Psa. 110:7). In the Psalm the Victor is described as "filling with bodies" as in a battlefield triumph (Psa. 110:6). In

Ephesians, Paul (who knows how Christ has conquered him to become his bondslave) turns the phrase to say that Christ fills his body, the church, "the fulness of him that filleth all in all" (Eph. 1:23).

Jesus Christ is glorified as the Servant with a glory that can be his only because he is also the eternal Son, the effulgence of God's glory and the very image of his substance (Heb. 1:3).

The Old Testament records God's dealings with his covenant people. The initiative is always with the Lord. He calls Abraham and promises that in him all the nations will be blessed. He appears to Moses at the burning bush and promises to deliver Israel from bondage in Egypt. He leads the people through the divided waters of the sea and brings them on eagles' wings to himself. At Sinai he binds them to him in his covenant; he leads them in the fiery cloud to the land of promise. When Israel breaks his covenant and worships idols in the house where God has set his name, God brings judgment. The people are carried into captivity and the smoke of destruction hangs over the courts of the Lord. But God's promises do not go up in smoke. The Old Testament prophets look forward to the latter days when all the promises of blessing will be realized. The people will be brought back from captivity; a remnant will be spared, and God will circumcise the hearts of his people. God will make a new covenant with a renewed people and all the ends of the earth will see the glory of the Lord.

How can all this come about? God himself must come to be the Deliverer of his people. The need of the people is so great that only God can meet it. Israel's hope is dead and gone. The prophet sees the people as dry bones scattered in the valley (Ezek. 37:1–14). Only the Spirit of God can assemble the scattered bones and give them resurrection life.

Further, the promises of God are so great that only

God can fulfill them. God promises not only peace and security but new hearts, life from the dead, a renewed universe.

God condemns the false shepherds that have exploited the flock. He will come himself to be the true Shepherd (Ezek. 34:11). God deplores the failure of Israel's false kings. He will put on the helmet of salvation and the breastplate of righteousness to be the Savior of his people (Isa. 59:17).

Isaiah sees the Lord coming again through the wilderness, leading the last great exodus of the people of God: "Prepare ye in the wilderness the way of Jehovah; make level in the desert a highway for our God" (Isa. 40:3). Then, amazingly, the coming of the Lord is linked to the coming of the Servant. "For unto us a child is born, unto us a son is given; and the government shall be upon his shoulder: and his name shall be called Wonderful, Counsellor, Mighty God, Everlasting Father, Prince of Peace" (Isa. 9:6).

The message of the New Testament is that the Lord has come. The angels sing, "Unto you is born this day in the city of David, a Saviour, which is Christ the Lord" (Luke 2:11, KJV). John the Baptist heralds the coming of Jesus with the words of Isaiah, "Make ye ready the way of the Lord" (Matt. 3:3). The One who comes is, as Simeon said, "The glory of thy people Israel" (Luke 2:32).

Jesus Christ the God-man ascends to enter into the glory which he had with the Father before the world was (John 17:5). He has "become by so much better than the angels, as he hath inherited a more excellent name than they" (Heb. 1:4). Born of the seed of David according to the flesh he is "over all, . . . blessed forever" (Rom. 1:3, 4; 9:5).

Do you sometimes wish that you could have walked with Jesus on the road to Emmaus? Would that seminar that Jesus conducted give you the key to interpreting the

Scriptures? Do you say, "Oh, if we could only have heard Jesus then! Our hearts would have burned within us. Our eyes would have been opened. But we weren't there, and Cleopas had no TV camera, or even a tape recorder. Jesus interpreted his sufferings and glory from the whole Old Testament but that interpretation is forever lost."

No, friends, we are in no such position as that. Jesus gave the Holy Spirit to the New Testament apostles and prophets as his witnesses. The whole New Testament gives us Jesus' interpretation of the Old. The teaching of Jesus in the forty days after his resurrection is not lost to the church. It is spread on the pages of the New Testament. That is why you find every page sprinkled with Old Testament quotations and allusions. The teaching of our Lord concerning himself is the teaching of the Scriptures.

We cannot separate our Lord Jesus Christ from the Bible. If we turn away from the Scriptures, and suppose that we are turning to Christ, then what we turn to is not the Christ of the Scriptures but a myth of our own imagination. If we turn to the Christ of the Scriptures, then we turn to the One who is the fulfillment of all the Scriptures: Moses and the prophets and the Psalms. We turn to the One who is himself the Lord of the Scriptures. We come to know him "whom to know aright is life eternal." If we do not have the Book that Jesus had, then we do not have the Lord that Book proclaims. But if we have the Lord, we also have the Book; for it is *his* Book, inspired by his Spirit, fulfilled by his life, his death, his resurrection, and his glory.

ROBERT C. PREUS is president of Concordia Theological Seminary in Fort Wayne, Indiana, and was previously an associate professor at Concordia Seminary in St. Louis, Missouri. He is a graduate of the University of Minnesota, Luther Theological Seminary, Edinburgh University, and Strasbourg University in France. He is the author of *The Inspiration of Scripture* and *The Theology of Post-Reformation Lutheranism.*

SCRIPTURE: GOD'S WORD AND GOD'S POWER

2 TIMOTHY 3:14–17

ROBERT C. PREUS

I'd like to begin with a hymn which is the form of a prayer.

Thus, O Jesus, my endeavor is to be forever Thine.
Let no mortal love whatever hindering now my heart entwine.
Though great be the host that refuses to heed Thee,
I'll faithfully follow where e'er Thou wilt lead me.
For Thy Word is Spirit and life to my soul,
And through it, O Jesus, my conduct control.

I want to comment on 2 Timothy 3:14–17. In our day of virtual worldwide revolution and insecurity, the most abiding thing that you and I can possess, and certainly the greatest legacy we can leave our children, is knowledge. By excessive taxation or by simple confiscation, everything we have can be taken from us—our income, our capital, our wealth, even our property. And this is actually happening in various places in the world.

Bible quotations are from the King James version, unless otherwise noted.

The last thing that can be taken from a person is what he has in his head. If we know something, we can usually make a way for ourselves even under very difficult circumstances and can at least exist. And the more we know, the better our lives will be. It was a man wise in the ways of this world who once said, "With all thy getting, get understanding." But knowledge not only prepares us for our brief life here on earth. There is a higher knowledge that opens doors of eternal life to us, and this is the knowledge of our Lord Jesus Christ. "This is life eternal," he says, "that they might know thee, the only true God, and Jesus Christ whom thou hast sent."

Now what does it mean to know Jesus Christ? It means not merely that I have a few facts at hand concerning his life and his death. It means not merely that I regard him as a great teacher, a martyr, an example, or even one who by his death and life has revealed God's love to me. To know Jesus Christ means to know his benefits—to know what he has done for me. To know him means to say to him, "My Lord, my God, my Savior."

And where do we gain this knowledge that leads to eternal life—the knowledge that Paul is talking about in these words? How do we learn to know Jesus Christ? How may we learn to recognize that communion with God, the forgiveness of sins, the sure hope of eternal life which we have when we know him? The answer is simple and clear: through his Word. Just as Christ himself is Life and Light, the words he has spoken are Spirit and Life. Just as he is the foundation of our life with God, so his Word is the foundation of our knowledge of that life which is to be had in God. And this Word through which we believe is, as he himself has said, "The Word of the apostles and the prophets," the Word of Holy Scripture.

As you know, Scripture makes many statements and

claims about itself—its power, authority, and divine origin. But most of these statements are brief; they are said only in passing. Of all the statements about itself, our text is by far the longest, the clearest, and the most complete. And it offers, I believe, three reasons why the Bible ought to be a most precious treasure to the church and to every Christian: First, because it is a powerful Word. Second, because it is a divine Word. Third, because it is an authoritative and practical Word.

In the opening words of this text, Paul is urging Timothy, his younger co-worker, to hold fast and to continue in everything that he has been taught by Paul and the other apostles. And the apostle reminds Timothy that everything he has taught him, Timothy has already learned or was supposed to have learned from the Scriptures, the same Scriptures which he learned as a child from his pious mother and grandmother. And why is it so important, so paramount that Timothy continue faithfully in the doctrine of Scripture? Is it simply so that he may remain loyal to a heritage, a culture? Is it to remain merely well-informed concerning God and his people and their history? Not that. No, Paul says there is an infinitely more important reason. Scripture, he says, is power. "It is able to make wise unto salvation through faith which is in Christ Jesus." Now just what is meant by this power of Scripture? What kind of a power does Scripture possess?

In the Middle Ages certain monks would strap a Bible to their backs thinking that it would aid them wherever they went and ward off evil spirits. Ironically, many of these monks were not even able to read the Bible. Certainly this is not the power of Scripture. The power of Scripture is not a fetish; it is not something magical.

Today many scholars who have a high respect for the Bible tell us that it is unique in this respect: it is the first authentic, original witness to Christ and therein is its power. But certainly, there is more to be said about the power of Scripture, God's Word, than merely that. We don't venerate the Bible simply because it's old. No, the power of Scripture is in its message. And its message is Christ. He is the essence, the soul, and the center of all the Scriptures.

As Luther used to say, "Christ is involved in the Scriptures as a body in its clothes." Scripture teaches us, Paul says; it makes us wise by teaching Christ: his atoning life, his suffering, his death—and placarding him before our eyes. And for every penitent sinner, this is a message of greatest comfort. It can fill the most despondent, wretched, miserable heart with peace and joy and hope, because it tells every sinner of the Savior, a Savior from sin, crucified and slain and risen. He is a Savior God who thrusts himself into our world, our misery, our death, our sin, our hell, taking our place, and then offers us forgiveness and reconciliation and righteousness and salvation—eternal rescue.

When we embrace this message of Scripture, as Paul says, "We become wise." Not just because we have acquired a little more factual knowledge. No, Paul tells us that this message of Scripture comes, "Not only in word, but also in power and in the Holy Spirit and with full conviction" (1 Thess. 1:5, RSV). It is God's power unto salvation. It not only informs; it seizes us; it changes us; it makes us new creations, children of God. Therefore, you must never forget these words of our text, the clearest words of all Scripture that talk about its power, and you must never minimize them.

"The Scriptures," Paul says here, "the *Scriptures.*" He is not speaking about some other kind of Word of God. The Scriptures are able; they have the intrinsic, inherent power, the power of very God to make you or me or any man wise unto salvation by bringing us to faith in Christ. And we must understand the full implication of what Paul is saying here. Scripture does this. Scripture is not merely a billboard or a sign that points to Christ the way some sign in Fort Wayne may point to Chicago. No, it brings Christ to me, and me to Christ; me, a poor, lost, dead sinner to Christ. That's the power of Scripture, what the living Word of Scripture does. Whether it is read or preached it does no less than what the living Word of Christ accomplished in dead Lazarus. It has given us life.

And so there is a good reason for singing as we do in another of our old hymns:

Speak, O Lord, thy servant heareth.
To Thy Word I now give heed.
Life and spirit Thy Word beareth.
All Thy Word is truth, indeed.
Death's dread power in me is rife.
Jesus, may Thy Word of life
Fill my soul with love's song's fervor,
That I cling to Thee forever.

Now, perhaps you are asking: How can Scripture, a book, be so powerful? And Paul in our text seems to anticipate just such a question. In giving an answer, he gives us an important second reason why the Scriptures should be such a great treasure to you and me and the entire Christian church. He says simply, "All Scripture is given by inspiration of God"—all Scripture is God-breathed; it is the product of God's breath. Here Paul tells us that Scripture is not the product of men. It's not the result of human ingenuity or thought or decision, even though, obviously, men wrote it, consciously and willingly. No, he says, Scripture is God's breath, the product of God's mouth, God's utterance. It came from his mouth, his heart, his will.

It's not a hodgepodge that reflects the theology of Isaiah or Paul or James or John or others. It teaches one theology, the theology that comes from God and reflects his mind and his will toward us. This is a very difficult concept for many people to accept today—even many theologians, as you know. Many are telling us that God is not the author of the Bible at all, but rather in some sense the author of the lives of the men who wrote the Bible and that is all that inspiration really means.

Paul says "no" to this. He does not even mention the human authors of the Scriptures, even though he was one of them. He was conscious of it as he was writing this. But he simply tells us that the Scriptures, as such—those Scriptures that we have at hand—are God-breathed. And so Luther is perfectly right when in his entire exegetical enterprise throughout his life, he simply said, "You are so to deal with Scripture that you bear in mind that God himself is speaking to you there."

The Bible is powerful to work faith in us—to make us wise unto salvation simply because it is God's Word. What a tragedy then, what a stupid, utter tragedy ever to toss that Book of books in the corner and just let it gather dust. Or in our theological studies to relegate that Book and what it says to some lower priority in all of our work. On the other hand, what a joy and what a comfort to know that whenever you take that Book up and read it, whenever you hear it expounded or preached, whenever you meditate on it, God himself is present, speaking to you.

The church fathers used to call the Scriptures *Deos loquam,* "God speaking." Not merely something God has said, but rather *God speaking now,* mediating to you his Son, his Holy Spirit, his forgiveness, all the riches of his grace. And why shouldn't that be a joy and a comfort to us? You and I, living in this fallen, cursed, perishing world can understand the psalmist when he said, "All men are liars." You and I can have the confidence that even though we never see God, he nevertheless speaks to us in the Bible, as directly and personally and with the same truth and power that he spoke to Adam in the Garden of Eden, or to Abraham on the field of Mamre. Moses, who spoke with God face to face; the disciples who sat at the feet of the Son of God and learned his message for three years have no advantage over you and me. You see now what it means, what the implications are when we say, "The Scriptures are God's Word."

And of course, when we say the Scriptures are God's Word we mean also that this powerful, saving Word is truthful, inerrant. This is obviously Paul's understanding in our text. The power of Scripture which Paul alludes to resides in its message and in the fact that it is God's Word. This message is the truth. It's a message which makes us wise unto salvation and free. It is quite impossible that this powerful, divine Word which Paul talks about here, which alone, as he says later, "is profitable for doctrine" in the church—that this Word could mislead us or contain errors of any kind. It is quite impossible that the cognitive message of the Scripture-word, which teaches us everything that God would have us believe and do, would mislead us at any point. If Paul doesn't say this explicitly, it is built right into his thinking as he makes these statements about Scripture. If not, how then could Paul possibly go on in this same text and say that Scripture is profitable and useful for so many things? Yet that is exactly what he does.

This is the third reason why the Scriptures should be so precious to us: because they are so imminently practical. Practical for everything that pertains to the Christian faith and life. Because the Bible is produced by the breath of God, Paul says, because it is his word, it is useful, profitable for the four things he lists. I am sure he could have listed many more, and there is a great deal of overlap among these four things.

First for doctrine, teaching. The Bible teaches a person the Christian faith. It teaches him what he's to believe, teach, and confess as a Christian. And certainly we Christians are not going to pooh-pooh doctrine, even in a subjectivistic age like ours.

Second, the Bible is profitable for reproof. What this means is that the Scriptures convince a person of their message. It is like Jerome's translation. The Bible, he says, "is profitable for arguing" in the positive sense. The Scriptures authenticate their own message. They prove themselves; this is what Paul is saying here.

Third, they are profitable for correction. This is a Greek word which comes from the same root as our word "orthodox." If you deviate in your morals, life, or doctrine, Scripture is there always to help you revise and amend your wrong ideas and life. It straightens you up.

Fourth, instruction in righteousness. Righteousness: the way in which we are to live. Scripture trains us, educates us in the way we are to walk as children of God, whether we are a Timothy or a layperson. In short, Paul tells us, in the Bible God teaches us all that we are to believe and do. And notice that Paul says that Scriptures make the man of God perfect; that is an old English word which really means totally equipped. It makes every man of God equipped in every direction, fully prepared for every exigency, fully informed for every emergency of life or death. Notice that nothing else is mentioned; *sola Scriptura,* Scripture alone. When you are instructed by Scripture, Paul tells you, you are instructed completely. Completely fitted for the Christian life. Just think of that. Paul uses the strongest possible words. He uses what we call "pleonasm," redundancy for the sake of emphasis. He says, "Timothy, you will be perfectly equipped. Yes, totally and perfectly equipped for every good work."

What the apostle is obviously trying to tell us here is simply that the Bible is the most practical book in the world. God has made it one book for all ages and all nations. It commends itself to every intellectual capacity, to every cultural setting, to every human necessity. It sets forth the spiritual truth and saving doctrine to all men, great and small, learned and simple, good and bad. And all men can understand it; by the gift of the Holy Spirit, they can embrace it and love it and live in it. One of the most moving testimonies concerning the Scriptures and their usefulness which I ever read was written years ago by Daniel Marsh, the well-known New England preacher and hymn writer. He says:

The Bible is the oldest and newest of books. It surveys the whole field of time and it looks furthest into the infinite depths of eternity. It lends the most vivid and absorbing interest to the scenes and events of the past and it keeps us in the most active sympathy in the time in which we live. It gives us the most reliable record of what has been and it affords us our only means of what is yet to be. It is so conservative as to make it the solemn duty to study and revere the past and it is so progressive as to be in advance of the most enlightened age. It is strict enough to denounce the very shadow and semblance of sin and it is liberal enough to save the chiefest of sinners. It is full of God and must, therefore, be read with a pure heart or its true glory will not be seen. It is full of man, and therefore must always be interesting and instructive to all who would know themselves. The Bible is the plainest of books and yet it has depths of wisdom which no created mind can sound. It is set up as a beacon to show all wanderers the safe way, and yet its light shines forth from thick clouds of mystery and from abysses of infinite darkness. It describes all conditions of life. And it gives utterance to all desires and emotions of the soul. It has a song of triumph for the victor and a wail of defeat for the vanquished. It sparkles with the fervor and gladness of youth; it celebrates the strength and glory of manhood. It bewails the sorrows and infirmities of age. It exalts the mighty deeds of kings and conquerors. It sympathizes with the poor and lowly. It lifts up the fallen. It delivers the oppressed and it breathes the blessing of peace upon the quiet homes of domestic life. It describes with startling clearness the seductions, the temptations, the conflicts of doubt and the miseries of scepticism. It searches the secret chambers of the heart and brings to light its purest love, its darkest hate, its highest joy and its deepest grief. It compasses the utmost range of thought and feeling and desire and it sounds the utmost depths of motive of character and passion.

I think Marsh catches in part what Paul is driving at when he says, "All Scripture is useful." God's Word is our great heritage.

And yet how we neglect and abuse this Word. And how we waste our time—yes, even as theologians—on other things. Already in his day King Solomon said that in the making of books there is no end. And sometimes I am inclined to think that he knew only the half of it. It is much worse today. But most of these books are no good. They are either inane or they cater to our baser instincts or they tend to lead us astray. Yes, even theological books. But out of this welter of tragic darkness and confusion, the Bible still shines bright and clear. It not only informs me how to be a good husband, a good father, a good citizen. It not only teaches me good business principles, good morals, good taste. It gives me a new outlook on life: the heavenly viewpoint which no other book in the world can give. And it sets me on that way toward eternal life, the way of faith in Christ Jesus. The Bible brings God to me; it brings heaven to earth; it brings hope to my confusion, and grace into my life of sin and sorrow. It tells me the thoughts of God himself, his thoughts of peace toward me and not of evil. It reveals to me the hidden deep things of God's glory and grace. It is the Lord's staff, as David says, that "comforts me" in trouble, in distresses. It is my spiritual meat and drink which nourishes and strengthens me every day of my life, and greatest of all it unites me with my Savior.

And so we sing in the doxology:

Lord, Thy words are waters living,
Where I quench my thirsty need.
Lord, Thy words are breath, life-giving;
On Thy words my soul doth feed.
Lord, Thy words shall be my life
Through death's veil and dreary night.
Yea, they are my sword prevailing
And my cup of joy unfailing.

I would like to touch on the question of hermeneutics, the principles or rules for biblical interpretation found in our text.

Back in the third and fourth centuries the church was faced with a certain crisis, a centering in Christology, theology, the trinity, and so forth. In the fifth and sixth centuries the church faced the crisis of salvation by grace in opposition to all kinds of syncretism and Pelagianism and things like that, that practically denied the work of the Holy Spirit.

In the sixteenth century, as you know, it was the way of salvation that was the great crisis facing the church. And a sinner was justified by faith in Christ alone without the deeds of the law. This was the great discovery of the Reformation. In the last two centuries I think the crisis has really centered around the Bible, its authority, its inerrancy, its inspiration. But closely connected in the last generation has been this vexing problem of hermeneutics, because, as you know, a person in principle at least could hold to the inerrancy and authority of the Bible and still by the way he reads it reject some of its most cardinal truth. So we are facing a hermeneutical crisis today which I think we are going to have to consider in our ten years of activity as we deal with inerrancy and authority. I believe that our text gives us a great deal of insight as to the correct approach.

There are two kinds of hermeneutical principles, as

you know. The first kind deals with the Bible insofar as it is like all other literature. And thus you learn how, according to these rules, to parse sentences, analyze linguistic statements, detect figures of speech, genre types, and so forth just as you would in other literature.

There is another kind of hermeneutics common at least to some books, certainly peculiar to the Bible. Namely, that kind of hermeneutics in which the book itself gives you certain information about how you are to read it. It involves the kind of attitude and mindset you bring with you when you read the Scriptures. Our text, I believe, mentions these things. Let me list just six of them.

The first one is what I might call the "unity principle." This is brought out in the very first two verses of our text, where Paul begins by telling Timothy to remain steadfast in the things which he has learned and been assured of, knowing from whom he has learned them. Now whether the Greek text is plural or singular there, I don't think it makes any difference. It means that Timothy is being reminded once again by Paul to stand fast in what Paul has taught him. It is at least the third time he has urged this in this very Epistle. No sooner does he complete that thought than he immediately goes to the Scriptures and says, "Now, Timothy, from a child you have known the Scriptures."

In other words, what Paul has taught him, Timothy already understood, at least in part, from the Scriptures, which had been taught him from childhood by his mother and grandmother. What does that mean? The unity of the testaments. The unity between the prophetic Word and the apostolic Word. Paul alludes to this elsewhere in his writings. In Romans 1, you remember, he says that he was called and set apart to preach the gospel, which God himself had foretold or spoken about ahead of time through the prophets in the Old Testament. The same gospel, the same message. The unity of Scripture.

Now the very first biblical hermeneutical principle to go at the advent of the historical-critical method was the unity of Scripture. This is a historical fact. So it is of immense importance when you approach this Book that you understand that it is a unit and not some garbled hodgepodge of different theological opinions, spanning hundreds of years.

A second principle of hermeneutics which I believe can be derived from our text is *power.* We already talked about that a little bit. Scripture is able; it has power to do certain things. It's God's Word. It contains a saving message, and it has the power to convince people of that message. Certainly a person wants to know this about a book when he approaches it. This is something that we should bear in mind always, that it is the almighty, everlasting, gracious, working, acting God who speaks to us and that his Word has power in our lives, great power. I think here of the story of the centurion that came to Jesus and asked that his slave who was at the point of death be healed, and Jesus said, "I'll come." "No, don't come. Speak the Word and my slave will be healed," he said. And Jesus spoke the word and his slave was healed. The same power resides in the Scripture which we read. Paul is referring to that. To pick up this Book and to read it with any other idea in mind really would be a great and tragic mistake.

The third hermeneutical principle is that the Scriptures have a soteriological purpose: their purpose is to bring a person to the point of conversion and salvation. Scripture is able to make you wise unto salvation, Paul says. In the reading of any book it is good if we can understand the motivation, the purpose of the writing. If you read Michener, for instance, he probably wants to entertain you, inform you a little bit, and maybe get in a little anti-Christian propaganda once in a while. It's well that you understand that when you read one of his books. There is a purpose in a stock market report; there is a purpose in the telephone book; there is a purpose in a sports story. Certainly nobody has to read these things without knowing ahead of time what their purpose is.

So also with the Bible. The Bible was written from beginning to end (remember that Paul here is talking primarily about the Old Testament—but we can include the New) in order that we might be saved. That's the word he uses here. That's the purpose of Scripture. If you miss this purpose as you read the Scriptures, obviously you are going to read them much to your detriment.

Fourth, I would use the word "Christocentricity." Maybe you don't think it is taught very clearly here, but I think it is. Scriptures are able to make us wise unto salvation through faith which is in Christ Jesus. This he says is the purpose of the Old Testament Scriptures as well as the New. It is obvious in the New to all of us. But this is also the purpose of the Old Testament, to witness to Christ. Christ, then, is the center of the Scriptures. That is the theme of all the Scriptures, and again when you approach a book you would like to know what the basic theme is. Of course you can get it inductively by reading the book. But it's helpful if you know this before you read it. And if you know that all of the book witnesses to Christ, then if you don't find him here or there you may search a little harder than ordinarily you would.

Fifth, the principle of divine origin: "All Scripture is given by inspiration of God." Every Scripture is God-breathed. It is good to know who the author is if you are reading a book which purports to be authoritative in any sense of the word. To know that the author is competent and authoritative himself means a great deal to you, whether he has written a book on history or ballistics or chemistry or whatever.

Now the author of this Book which deals totally with God and Christ, is God himself. I think a word ought to be said about the Greek words *pasa graphe.* The *pasa* is distributive. The *pasa.* It probably ought to be translated "every Scripture." It can't be collective; then it would be *pasa he graphe.*

Paul is not merely saying that Scripture as a whole is God-breathed in some sense, but that every Scripture is God-breathed. He is teaching verbal inspiration. That is not a conclusion drawn from anything; it is taught here. And that, of course, shows us that we must meticulously watch all the words and phrases of Scripture and read it in that sense; the way, of course, the Christian church has done historically through the ages.

And finally, authority or usefulness. Scripture has a usefulness that is always valuable to us because it is God's Word and bears with it his authority. And notice the connection. You could really translate verse 16 by saying, "All Scripture is God-breathed, or every Scripture is God-breathed and is therefore profitable because of its divine origin. Its authority guarantees its total usefulness for you and me and the entire Christian church." Authoritative so that we can trust it in every respect. And that too is something important as you take up a book to read. Is it authoritative? Can you count on it? Must you obey it and believe its message, or not?

The following hymn certainly typifies everything Paul is saying in this magnificent text. It was written by a Dane named Grundvig:

God's Word is our great heritage,
And shall be ours forever.
To spread its light from age to age
Shall be our chief endeavor.
Through life it guides our way;
In death it is our stay.
Lord, grant while worlds endure
We keep its teaching pure
In every generation.

JAMES M. BOICE is pastor of the historic Tenth Presbyterian Church in Philadelphia, Pennsylvania, and speaker on The Bible Study Hour Radio Program, heard weekly across the United States. He attended Harvard College, Princeton Theological Seminary, and completed doctoral studies in Basel, Switzerland. He has written twenty books. Dr. Boice is Chairman of the International Council on Biblical Inerrancy.

THE MARKS OF THE CHURCH
JOHN 17:17
JAMES M. BOICE

It would be impossible with a goal such as ours in this conference to overlook that great text on Scripture found in the middle of the Lord's prayer for his church, John 17:17: "Sanctify them by the truth; your word is truth." In a conference dealing with inerrancy a text like that should be expounded at some length.

What I'd like to do, however, is to treat it not merely by itself, but in its context. In this second half of our Lord's prayer we have a series of requests by the Lord Jesus Christ on behalf of his church to the effect that God the Father would grant to the church those distinguishing marks which are to set it apart from the world around it. As he prays he mentions these in sequence, linking each one to the truth or to the Scriptures, which is the same thing.

In the broader context, when we consider that this has to do as well with the character of Christ, I believe we have three things working together. We have the Word of God, the Scriptures. We have the characteristics or

Bible quotations are from the *New International Version.*

marks of the church here enumerated. And we have the character of Christ. Our Lord possesses these characteristics intrinsically. Now he prays that those marks which are true of him might also be true of us, and the medium through which this might come to pass is the Word.

The marks listed, beginning in verse 13, are these. First of all, joy. Jesus prays that his joy might be fulfilled in us in full measure. Second, holiness. Jesus refers to this as sanctification. Third, there is the matter of truth itself, undoubtedly involving doctrinal matters in this context. Fourth, there is mission. Fifth, unity. Last of all, at the very end of the prayer, our Lord brings forth the great characteristic of love. Now as he was joyful, so are we to be joyful. As he was sanctified (and he prays for that), so are we to be sanctified. As he was characterized by truth, so is our life together to be characterized by truth. As he was sent into the world, so are we sent into the world. As he and the Father are one, so are we to be one. And as he loved and demonstrated that love fully at the cross, so are we to love those others to whom we are sent. Those are the marks.

I don't know what you think of when a series of characteristics like this is mentioned, but I must admit that when I look at that first mark "joy," the question that comes to my mind is, "Why should that be there at all?" Or again, "Why should it be in first place?" If someone had asked me, before I gave any serious attention to this chapter, "What are the distinguishing marks of the church?" I'm sure I would have said in the first instance, "doctrinal faithfulness." Second, I might have said, "Love." In third place I might have gotten to some of these other characteristics. But I know that I would never have placed joy in first place and would, in fact, probably never even have thought of it. Why does Jesus mention this first when he is talking about that which should characterize his people upon earth?

I think it's really not too difficult to answer this question. It's not that joy is the greatest mark of the church. Love is that. Perhaps the point is not even that joy is what we most need. That's a question that has to be answered in a different way in different periods of church history, depending upon the state of the church in those periods. Joy is not even first in the sense that it is foundational. The interlinking of these marks of the church clearly indicates that it is the Word of God, the truth of God, that's foundational. Joy is in first place because it is the first thing we notice in the life of those who come to faith in Christ. Joy is present when they respond to the grace of God in the gospel through saving faith.

We preach the gospel to people who are burdened by sin and troubled by uncertainty. They don't know which way to turn. They don't know what to think. They worry about the future. They don't know who they are. As the law convicts them, they sense that they are not in a right relationship with God. But then the gospel comes. They believe it, are transformed and joy fills their hearts.

We can think further and recognize that joy characterized the early church. It was a joyful assembly. That word joy in its verbal form, *chairein,* is found seventy-two times in the pages of the New Testament. The noun form of the word *chara* is found sixty times. As you study these references you find that they do not involve some carefully worked out theological statement in which true joy is distinguished from the false. Rather, joy occurs in a natural way on the lips of Christians in normal everyday intercourse, as they say to one another, "Greetings in the Lord. Be joyful. Rejoice. Joy be with you," and phrases such as these. Such were common greetings in New Testament times.

It is true that we also find this word on the lips of pagans. The letter written on behalf of Paul by Felix the

Roman Governor begins with this word. We translate it perhaps most accurately today as "Greetings." Yet the word occurs in specific Christian contexts as, for example, when the birth of Jesus is announced and the angels say to the shepherds, "I bring you good news of a great joy which will be to all people." Or Paul, writing to the Philippians in a letter literally overflowing with joy, says toward the end of the fourth chapter, "Rejoice in the Lord, and again I say, rejoice."

Let us stop here and ask if that is true of us. Is that true of the churches we know? Is it true of our assembly here? Well, many times it is. But at other times, I think we must admit, it also is not. You know that bit of doggerel written years ago in Scotland by a man who must have been listening to a dry Scottish sermon. He was doodling during the sermon, and then he set to writing verses. After the service was over the janitor found this poem: "To dwell above with saints in love, aye that will be glory. To dwell below with saints I know, now that's a different story." And it is!

Another of our hymn writers, one of the Wesleys, has written, "Our souls can neither rise nor go to reach eternal joy." That is a sad commentary on the way things often are. Instead of the joy that should characterize the lives of those who are reconciled to God by the death of Christ, we have long faces and seem to project misery to our contemporaries.

What is the solution? If joy is lacking, what should be done? The answer is in this verse itself, as well as being written into the entire fabric of the Word of God. Notice what our Lord says, "I am coming to you now, but I say these things while I am still in the world, so that they have the full measure of my joy within them." In other words, the answer to the problem of a lack of joy is the teaching of Jesus Christ.

You find the same point in the fifteenth chapter, verse eleven. There Jesus is speaking again and says, "I have told you this so that my joy may be in you." The next verse, verse fourteen, goes on to say, "I have given them your word." So Christ's reference to joy is bracketed by references to the Scriptures.

If we ask, how is it that the Scriptures lead us to joy? the answer is that they bring us to a knowledge of God in whom we can be joyful. They teach us of the character of God and of those acts in which he has reached out in mercy to save us. He has brought us out of darkness into his marvelous light. If we aren't joyful about that, if we don't literally overflow with enthusiasm for that kind of a salvation, then we don't understand it very well and need to get back into the pages of the Word of God, so that God might teach us about it more fully.

Second, our Lord mentions holiness or sanctification (v. 17). "Sanctify them by the truth; your word is truth." I think we have difficulty when we talk about holiness or sanctification in that we begin at the wrong end of things. When we talk of sanctification we tend naturally to begin with the matter of moral conduct or righteousness. But while it is true that conduct or righteous acts have much to do with sanctification, we distort the idea when we begin at that point. Because holiness is that which is characteristic, above all, of God, and God's holiness at its root is not so much an ethical righteousness but rather what we would best call "transcendence."

It is that which sets God apart. He is other than us in his holiness. Therefore, when we talk about sanctification on the human level, what we must talk about first of all is being consecrated or separated unto God. This is the only thing that makes sense of this particular passage moreover. Because our Lord in verse nineteen, just after he has prayed for our sanctification, prays about himself saying, "For them I sanctify myself, that they too may be truly sanctified." If he is thinking here of becoming more righteous in the way we normally think of that term, of becoming more holy, more intrinsically right, then he would be saying that he is less than fully holy as he prays. Obviously we are on the wrong track when we begin to think that way.

What Jesus is saying is, "I consecrate myself, I set myself apart to the great work that you have given me." That work was the death on the cross which was to come shortly after this. It is in this sense that we must understand him to be praying for us, and this means that he was asking that we might be set apart to the purposes of God. This involves our wills, our priorities, our conception of life, our desires—all those things. And if we ask again, "But how do we become thus sanctified? Is it through an emotional experience? Is it through group interaction? Is it by consensus?" None of these things is given by the Lord as the answer. The answer is *by thy truth.* It is as we take up the Word, read it, study it, as we "inwardly digest" its teachings, as the old Scottish phraseology says, that God speaks to us and himself separates us unto the work he has for us to do.

Today we need a church that is sanctified in that sense—set apart to the work, character and desires of God and not to the desires of men, even though they are sometimes sanctified in a secular way by ecclesiastical garb.

Third, we come to truth itself, that which lies at the base of the other two and indeed is related to the marks which follow later on in the chapter. Here you have a great emphasis upon it. Jesus mentions his teaching, God's Word, the truth itself—all obviously expressions of the same thing—and his prayer is that God might use this to sanctify us. He wants us to be established in the truth.

Now we have a problem at that point, and we have to confess it. We talk about the Word of God as truth. We are right to do so. But we have to acknowledge when we speak along those lines that the world of our day no longer strictly believes in truth. The great apologists of our time are all saying that. C. S. Lewis said it very well in the opening pages of *The Screwtape Letters,* where the devil's henchman, tempting his patient on earth, is advised not to talk about truth and falsehood because people don't operate on that basis anymore, but rather to talk about what's useful or what's practical. "That's the way to get through," says the devil.

Francis Schaeffer has said the same thing in more philosophical terms. He's pointed out quite rightly that today, unlike previous generations, people, though they speak of truth and falsehood, are not speaking of truth in the biblical sense or even in the traditional sense to mean that which is true now and will always be true universally. Rather they mean that which is true now but not necessarily tomorrow or yesterday; or it is true for me but not necessarily for you. In other words, truth for contemporary men and women is relative.

But here we have truth embodied in the Scriptures and undoubtedly to be lived out in the lives of believers as a great mark of the church. And when we consider the world out there that, strictly speaking, doesn't believe in truth, we ask, "How are we to operate on such a basis? What are we to do?"

Here the efficacy of the Word of God comes in: the fact that God really uses the Word to accomplish his purposes, whether men and women believe in the Word of truth or not. Take a person who is first exposed to the preaching of the gospel. He doesn't really believe there is any such thing as truth. The gospel is preached, and his initial reaction is simply: "That's all right for you; you can believe that if you want." He won't argue with you, but he feels that there's no reason why the gospel should be true for him. And yet because he lacks knowledge of the truth, his own life doesn't come together. Even in an area where he thinks he's coping, things don't quite jell. He can't understand his own personality. There are problems that he can't cope with. There's the future, death. These things he fears.

But then the Word of God is preached. He doesn't believe in the truth, but the truth is preached and as God, who is himself truth, speaks to the heart of the individual through the Spirit of truth, the truth gets hold upon him. Then the various parts of his life begin to fall into place, and he recognizes that he now has something like a key to knowledge. That which he didn't understand about himself and life now begins to make sense.

As we take these marks of the church and speak, as we must, of joy, sanctification, and truth, we recognize that at this point Christ's thinking is moving to our relationship to the world as well. He is saying to us, "Now when you go, when you speak, when you testify, don't forget that the basis of your testimony and the means by which it will be effective is my Word embodied in the Scriptures."

That is a bridge for us to the fourth mark of the church, this matter of mission. Jesus says, "As you sent me." The Latin word *mitto (mittere, misi, missum),* from which we get our word mission, means "to send." He is saying, "As you sent me into the world, so have I sent them into the world." Think of that in the sequence of Jesus' statements. We have spoken of joy, sanctification, and truth. We have spoken of them as marks of the church, things that we should have and yet don't have in the fullest measure. We ask God to develop these in us. But when we begin to think of these things we realize that we could have joy, sanctification, and truth in fullest measure much more quickly if God simply translated us all into heaven. We have joy here, it is true. But what is that compared to the joy we'll have when we see God face to face? In that day in heaven there will be no tears, no parting from loved ones.

Or concerning this matter of sanctification: by the grace of God, we are consecrated unto him. We realize a degree of ethical righteousness. But certainly we fall short of what Christ would have us be. How about that day when we'll see Christ and be like him? Couldn't God sanctify us quicker by taking us home to be with him?

Or again, concerning truth: why can we not be brought into the presence of God and know no longer through a mirror darkly, but fully, face to face?

The reason why that is not the way God operates is found in this fourth mark, mission. God has left us in the world in order that we might be witnesses to the world, just as he sent his beloved Son into the world to be a witness to the world. This text tells us a great deal about the church's mission. One thing it tells us is that we are *sent into the world.* It doesn't say that we are to be of the world, but it does say that we are to be in the world. One of the great weaknesses of the evangelical church is that we have been in the business of building up walls to keep us isolated from the world.

A friend of mine says that we have constructed our Christian ghetto society in such a way as to make it possible to go through all of life and never touch the world at all. You can be born in a Christian home of Christian parents, go to a Christian day school, followed by a Christian college, followed by a Christian graduate school. When you finish those you can go to work for a Christian company and join a Christian club (known as a church). You can even see Christian movies for entertainment. When you get sick you can be attended by a Christian doctor and eventually, I suppose, die and be buried by a Christian undertaker in hallowed ground.

In contrast, we can't help but be impressed by the fact that the Lord moved out to where the people were. He touched their hands; he mingled in their crowds. He made friends of the outcasts, so much so that it was brought up as a slur on his reputation. They said, "Look how he behaves." But he did it in order that he might win people.

There's a second thing that needs to be said about that phrase. Jesus says, "I sent them into the world as you have sent me into the world," and that means not only that we are to be in the world, but that we are to be *as Christ* in the world. Many of us don't have any trouble going into the world; we can rub shoulders with the world and be like the world. We are fulfilling one half of Christ's commission, but in doing so we are missing the whole because we are not as Christ in the world. He says that we are to be like he is. What does this mean? Well, if the marks which he is giving the church are his marks, then we go into the world as joyful sons and daughters of the Most High, as set apart to God's purposes, as characterized by truth. As we read on we find that our lives are to be marked by unity and love as well. When we are so marked, God will bless our testimony.

It is unfortunate that we are often so much like the world. I have a friend whose wife, years ago, in order to earn a little bit of extra money and help them in the early days of their ministry, sold a well-known program for reducing. She got all the material and went out to sell this program, but she wasn't having much success. She came back to her husband and asked him what she was doing wrong. "Well," he said, "I don't know. Let me hear your speech." So she gave it. She explained what she said when she knocked on a door and how she presented the material. He said, "There's nothing wrong with that. It sounds perfectly all right. Let me see your literature." She gave him the literature and it seemed to be well printed. It was attractive. No problem. He was leafing through it and suddenly he said, "Oh, oh."

She asked, "Why are you saying, 'Oh, oh,' at a time like this?"

He said, "Do you want me to be truthful or tactful?"

She said, "Truthful, of course."

He said, "Dear, the trouble is that you look more like the picture before than the picture after."

Our difficulty as we go to the world as Christians is quite often that we are more like the picture before than the picture after. No wonder our Lord prayed that we might be characterized by these things.

Fifth, Jesus prays for unity. Unity is a hard thing to talk about, because there are so many conceptions of what unity should be. Some of them are wrong; some of them are partially wrong. Some people conceive of unity in organizational terms. They try to get all Christians together in one great big organization. We who are evangelicals tend to speak against that. We know that unity has to have some organizational expression. Yet we recognize rightly that an organizational unity in itself is not that for which Christ prayed.

As we look at the problem historically we can say rightly, I believe, that the greatest organizational unity the church ever had was in the period of the Middle Ages before the Reformation. But it was also the period of the church's greatest decadence. You had a church that was literally one wherever you went: north, east, south, or west. It was one church with the Pope at its head. Yet the results that Christ says are to follow, namely that if we are one, men and women will believe the gospel and come to him, didn't follow. In fact, thinking people had great difficulty even in believing in God, so great was the church's decadence. So when we talk about unity and recognize our obligation to be one, we recognize that, while our unity may have organizational aspects, that's certainly not what our Lord has in mind.

Evangelicals rest pretty easy at that point. We say, "Yes, that's true. That's what the liberal church is trying to do. We certainly stay away from that." But I think there's another error of which we are a little more guilty. It is to think of the unity for which Christ prayed as conformity. This is our problem, because we want to force Christians into an identical pattern. We want to look alike and function alike, I suppose as an ego-projection of who we are or consider ourselves to be.

But God is a God of variety. We see variety in nature. We see variety in the church. This is a wonderful gift to the church. So when our Lord speaks of unity as a mark of the church, he is certainly not encouraging us to force everybody into the same mold.

What is he praying for? As he himself explains it it is not at all difficult. What he's talking about is a unity analogous to the unity that exists within the Godhead. He makes that the pattern. He says, "As you and I are one [meaning Father and Son], so do I want them to be one." This unity is one of will, purpose, and direction. Our Lord is saying, "I want them to be like that. I want them to be of one mind, indeed of my mind, our mind. I want them to be united in their purpose, commitment, and other things."

As we look at Christ's prayer we recognize that this, as in the case of the other characteristics, is often not true of us. If it *is* to be true of us, we have a practical obligation of getting into the Word in order that the mind of Christ, which is revealed in Scripture, might by his grace increasingly be our mind as well.

If we look to ourselves, the diversity is there. Conflict is there. There is no opportunity of resolving these things. But if we look to the Word, in which we see the mind and purposes of God revealed, then that becomes the point at which our minds are transformed and we are drawn to one another.

Now we come to the last mark: love. As I said at the beginning, this is the greatest mark of all. Our Lord emphasizes love by placing it last. He prays this way, "I have revealed you to them, and will continue to make you known in order that the love you have for me may be theirs and that I myself may be in them" (v. 26). That is the point on which he ends. The Apostle Paul said the same thing in 1 Corinthians 13. There he is talking about faith, hope, and love. He gets to the end. He reflects on them. Then he says that these all abide—faith, hope, and love. They're lasting. But he acknowledges that "the greatest of these is love."

It occurs to me that you see the unique importance of this mark of the church when you imagine what it would be to subtract love from each of the other marks. Take joy, first of all, and subtract from it that holy love which is revealed in Jesus Christ. What do you have then? You have the kind of hedonistic reveling that is found in the secular world.

Take sanctification, and take love from that. You end up with self-righteousness, the kind of thing that characterized the Scribes and Pharisees of Christ's day, but allowed them to be filled with hatred, so much so that they crucified the Lord Jesus Christ when he came.

Take love away from truth. What do you have? You have what is called a bitter orthodoxy. It is the kind of teaching which is right but is proclaimed in such harsh terms that it doesn't win anybody.

Take love away from mission and you have colonialism, in which we work to win people for the sake of our own country or our own organization, whatever that may be.

Take love from unity and you have ecclesiastical tyranny, in which the church imposes its standards upon all who are within its community.

But look, if instead of subtracting love in that way, you express love—for God the Father, the Lord Jesus Christ, the Bible, one another, the world—what do you have? You have all these marks of the church, because they follow naturally upon it. When you express love for God, what happens? Your heart is filled with joy, because he is a great and marvelous God. What could be more joyful or a greater cause for rejoicing than fellowship with him? Express love for the Lord Jesus Christ and what happens? Sanctification follows, because, as he said, "If you love me you will keep my commandments." Express love for the Word, and you will be marked by truth. Express love for the world, and you will find yourself involved in mission. Love for one another will result in unity.

You see how it all ties together. It's really a very remarkable prayer, as we should expect from the lips of our Lord.

The only thing that needs to be said as we come to the end of this passage is that the only place we are ever going to find out about love and be made like Christ in his love, is in the pages of the Word of God. I don't know if you have noticed this, but I am sure you have at least thought along these lines: the love of God which is commended to us so fervently in the Scriptures is almost always linked to the cross of Jesus Christ.

It's true that you find the love of God expressed in the Old Testament, though not as strongly as in the New. It's true that you have it in Christ's teachings, because he taught that God loves us as a father loves his children. All of that is true. But there is no doubt that the supreme manifestation of the love of God is at the cross of Jesus Christ. Therefore, when you find the love of God explained, when you find the love of God commended, it's always done on this basis: "God so loved the world that he *gave* his only begotten Son."

If we find ourselves distant from God, we'll find our love for God and our sense of his love diminishing. But as we feed upon his Word, grow in its teaching, and share it as God gives us opportunity, then our love for him will grow. As our love for him grows, our love for others will grow. And these marks of the church which are so often sadly lacking in the communion of Christian people will increasingly mark us and our service for him.

W. A. CRISWELL has been pastor of the First Baptist Church in Dallas, Texas, for over thirty-five years. He is a graduate of Baylor University and holds a doctorate in philosophy from Southern Baptist Theological Seminary. He has written over thirty books and numerous articles, and has spoken literally around the world.

WHAT HAPPENS WHEN I PREACH THE BIBLE AS LITERALLY TRUE

W. A. CRISWELL

My subject is, "What happens when I preach the Bible as literally true." And I am presuming that the reason I have been chosen for such a topic is because I have been preaching for so long, pastoring a church, preaching the gospel now for over fifty-one years. I was reminded of that recently when at the dinner table after the service on Sunday, my little grandson indicated that in Sunday school he had just been taught about Noah and the flood. So at the dinner, in all sobriety, he said to me, "Granddaddy, did you know Noah?"

Well, I almost did. But not in all of my life have I had a subject assigned to me that pleased my own heart more fully and devoutly than this one. "What happens when I preach that the Bible is literally true?"

First, what happens to me personally? In believing and in studying and in preparing and in preaching that the Word of God is infallible and inerrant and inspired and literally true, I grow in the knowledge of God and in the image of Christ. Christ is identified with his Word. Both of them are called the Word of God. Revelation

Bible quotations are from the King James version.

19:11–13: "I saw heaven opened, and behold a white horse; and he that sat upon him was called Faithful and True . . . His eyes were as a flame of fire, and on his head were many crowns . . . He was clothed with a vesture dipped in blood: and his name is called The Word of God." John 1:1: "In the beginning was the Word, and the Word was with God, and the Word was God." Both of them are called the Word of God. Christ is identified with his Word. When I minimize the written Word, I dishonor the incarnate Word. But when I magnify the written Word I glorify the incarnate Word. God and his Word are one and the same. A man and his word may be two different things, but not God who is the same yesterday and today and forever.

When I love the Word of God, I love God. When I believe the Word of God, I believe God. When I preach the Word of God, I preach God. When I receive the Word of God. I receive God. And spiritually when I know the Word of God, I know God.

In my seminary days my Greek teacher was Dr. A. T. Robertson, the author of that tremendous Greek New Testament grammar. And after we had finished our course in the Gospels in the Greek New Testament, he held it up in his hand and said, "Young gentlemen, you have studied Christ himself. You have studied Jesus." Erasmus wrote in the preface to his Greek New Testament a word that went in summation like this: "On these pages you will find the living Christ and you will see Him more fully and more clearly than if He stood before you, before your very eyes." Christ and his Word are identified with each other. And when I love the written Word, I love the incarnate Word.

I am convicted by the Word of God. Hebrews 4:12, 13: "For the word of God is quick, and powerful, and sharper than any two-edged sword, piercing even to the dividing asunder of soul and spirit, and of the joints and marrow, and is a discerner of the thoughts and intents of the heart . . . but all things are naked and opened unto the eyes of him with whom we have to do."

I am born again. I am regenerated. I am saved by the Word of God; 1 Peter 1:23, 25 says: "Born again . . . by the word of God, which liveth and abideth for ever. And this is the word which by the gospel is preached unto you." James 1:18: "Of his own will begat he us with the Word of truth." John 15:3: "Now ye are clean through the word which I have spoken unto you." Ephesians 5:26: "That he might sanctify and cleanse it with the washing of water by the word."

No man is ever saved; no man is ever regenerated; no man is ever born again aside from the Word of God. In Acts 10 and 11 is a story of the Caesarean Gentile pentecost. An angel appeared before the Roman centurion saying, "Send men to Joppa for one Simon, whose surname is Peter: . . . he shall tell thee what thou oughtest to do" (Acts 10:5, 6). Why didn't the angel tell him how he and his house might be saved? Because no man is ever saved apart from the delivery of the Word of God. In keeping with the beautiful passage in Romans 10, "For whosoever shall call upon the name of the Lord shall be saved. How then shall they call on him in whom they have not believed? and how shall they believe in him of whom they have not heard? and how shall they hear without a preacher?" (v. 14). No man is ever saved apart from the delivery of the Word of God.

I am kept from sin by the Word of God. Psalm 119:11: "Thy word have I hid in mine heart, that I might not sin against thee." I am to walk by the Word of God. Psalm 119:105: "Thy word is a lamp unto my feet, and a light unto my path."

I am to live by the Word of God. Matthew 4:4: "Man shall not live by bread alone, but by every word that proceedeth out of the mouth of God."

And I am to die by the Word of God. Revelation 3:10: "Because thou hast kept the word of my patience,

I also will keep thee from the hour of temptation, which shall come upon all the world."

One of the beautiful women in our church married in New York City a man who all his life had lived a worldly existence producing plays on Broadway. They decided to move to Dallas and she brought him to church. And in attendance he found the Lord. He was beautifully converted. Then as he grew in grace, to my great sorrow he suddenly died of a heart attack. When I went to the funeral home to conduct the last and memorial service, I stood by his wife and looked into the casket on his still and silent face. He had in his hand a Bible. I turned to her in amazement and I said, "I've never seen that before. A man silent and still in death with his Bible in his hand."

She said, "When he was saved he sought to redeem the time and everywhere that Bible was with him. He'd prop it up," she said, "by the side of the mirror when he shaved his face in the morning. He'd always have it by his side when he drove in the automobile, and he'd take it to bed with him at night." And she said, "When the funeral director prepared his body and I looked upon his silent face, here in the casket his hands seemed so empty; the hands that had so often held that sacred Book." She said, "I went upstairs to the bedroom and I brought down his Bible and I put it in his hand."

When the service convened the next Lord's day morning in our church, I announced to the people that I had said to my wife that when I die and my body lies in the sanctuary of our dear church, I want them to place in my hand the Word of God as a last and living testimony to the truth of the everlasting promise of God.

And we are to preach the Word of God: 2 Timothy 3:16: "All scripture is given by inspiration of God." All Scripture is God-breathed. And what a tragedy that there is a chapter heading there. They go together. The next chapter, chapter four, verses one and two: "I charge thee therefore . . ." The "therefore" looks back to the great avowal and affirmation the prophet has just said. All Scripture is God-breathed, inspired by the breath of the Spirit of God. "I charge thee therefore before God, and the Lord Jesus Christ, who shall judge the quick and the dead at his appearing and his kingdom; preach the word. . . ."

Not, "thus saith Einstein," or "thus saith Smellfungus" or "thus saith Dr. Soundingbrass," or "thus saith Professor Guisedust," but, "thus saith the Lord God." That's the way the man is to preach. And our hope of our salvation and our assurance of heaven is found in the Word of God. John 5:24: "Verily, verily [truly, truly; amen, amen], I say unto you, he that heareth my word, and believeth on him that sent me, hath everlasting life, and shall not come into condemnation; but is passed from death unto life."

I was converted when I was ten years old in a little white crackerbox of a church house in a little town in far northwest Texas. I'd received permission from my parents to be excused from school and to attend the midweek service. And when I came into the little church I happened to be seated back of my old and sainted mother. When the preacher had done his message we stood up to sing, "There is a fountain filled with blood," and while we were singing that hymn of blood atonement my mother turned around and with many tears said to me, "Son, today will you take the Lord Jesus as your Savior?" I answered, "Mother, today, this day will I receive the Lord Jesus as my Savior." And I stepped out of the aisle and down to the front, hardly able to see the pastor for the tears in my own eyes.

I began preaching when I was seventeen years old, under tents, under arbors, out in the country in central west Texas and in Kentucky. And in those days, in what they called "camp revivals," they would have grove prayer meetings. The women would stay under the arbor, or under the tent, and the men would gather under a grove of trees and there they would testify of the grace of God and we would pray. I listened to those marvelous testimonies, and they were astonishing and miraculous to me.

For example, one of the men said, "See that spot right there. I had been under the burden of my sins for years and years, and as I stood in that spot, suddenly there came down from heaven a ball of fire that burst over my head and struck me to the ground." He said, "How long I lay in that state I do not remember, but when I stood to my feet. . . ." Then he described how the burden of sin had rolled away. And then he described how the birds sang, and how the trees were foliated, and how the mules plowed and all the other glorious and remarkable things that tend up to his miraculous conversion.

That's just typical of any endless number of them that I listened to. And I came to the conclusion in those days that I had not been converted. I was not born again. I was not regenerated. I was not a Christian. I had never seen a ball of fire. I had never seen an angel from heaven. I had never seen a light from glory. I had no marvelous experience to recount. And I came to the firm conclusion that I was not saved, that I was not a Christian.

I cannot describe to you the awful conflict in my heart in those years—not days and months, but years—when on Sundays I would stand up in my little country church and preach the gospel the best I knew how, and then every night, kneel down by the side of my bed and cry to God, "I haven't been saved. I'm not regenerated. I haven't been born again. I don't have any marvelous experience to recount. Lord, Lord, show me a light from heaven. Let a ball of fire burst over my head. Show me an angel of light."

Well, of course, in those days preaching the Bible I

read many things in it. One, I read in the Corinthian letter where Paul says that Satan transforms himself into an angel of light. And I read in Revelation 13, he sends fire down from heaven to deceive them upon the earth. And then, as time went by, things began to crystallize in my heart and it came about like this.

I can imagine someday standing in the great assize before the Judge of all the earth while the redeemed of God are marching in. I would assay to join their number and the Lord God would stop me and say, "By what right and by what prerogative do you enter my beautiful city and walk on my golden streets?" And I'd say, "Lord God, I know I'm saved; I know I'm a Christian; I know I have been born again. There came down from heaven a great ball of fire and it burst over my head. I know I'm saved." And Satan would laugh, "Ha, ha, ha. Listen to him. He saw a ball of fire. I sent that ball of fire just to deceive him." And he'd drag my soul down to hell. What could I say or what could I do? Or in that day when I stand in the great assize and the children of the redeemed are entering in, I imagine that the Lord God stops me and says, "By what right and by what prerogative do you go through my pearly gates and mingle with my sainted redeemed?" And I say, "Lord God, I know I'm a Christian; I know I'm saved; I saw an angel from heaven." And Satan would laugh, "Ha, ha, ha, ha, ha. He saw an angel from heaven. I transformed myself into that angel. Just to deceive him." And he'd drag my soul down to hell. What could I say or what could I do?

But truly, in that great assize when I stand before the Lord God and the redeemed of glory are entering in and the Lord God says to me, "By what right, by what prerogative do you enter my beautiful city and walk on my golden streets?" I'm going to say, "Lord God, when I was a boy ten years of age in a revival in a little white crackerbox of a church house in the town where I lived,

I went to a morning service and happened to be seated by my old and sainted mother. And when the preacher had done his sermon, my mother turned to me and said, 'Son, today will you receive the Lord Jesus as your Savior?' And I received the Lord Jesus the best a ten-year-old boy could. I took the Lord Jesus as my Savior. And blessed Jesus, all I'm doing, all I'm doing is just resting upon your words and your promise. For you said in John 1:12, 'As many as received him, to them gave he power [the authority, the prerogative, the privilege] to become the sons of God, even to them that believe on his name.' And Lord God, all I'm doing is just trusting in your Word and in your promise." Then I dare Satan to scoff, or to lie, or to ridicule. My salvation rests not upon some monstrous experience. My salvation rests upon the Word and promise of the Lord. And if he lies to me, and if he deceives me I'm lost, but if the promise of God in Christ is an everlasting, yea-and-amen, I'm safe; I'm born again, I'm a child of the King, and I'll see his face someday.

Preaching that the Bible is literally true, not only in my personal life, but in my sermon preparation, is a heavenly and daily and continual benediction. You see, I hear of preachers marching up and down in their studies, pacing back and forth; "What shall I preach; what shall I say?" I also in my study pace up and down. What shall I say? What shall I preach? But my problem is a little different. Mine is—Lord God, I am going to die before I even begin to get started to say everything that I have found in this blessed book. When I return to my study on Sunday night, I read the passages before me, those that pick up where I left off Sunday morning. Where I leave off Sunday night, I follow through the following Sunday morning. I am always preaching through a book in the Bible, and the text is always there before me. And because I preach that the Bible is literally true, exegesis is possible in my study and in my ministry. The man who is liberal and does not believe in the inerrant and inspired Word of God—to him exegesis is foolishness and folly. It's an anomalous situation that he could stand up there and exegete a passage which he doesn't believe is inspired. That would be impossible for me. You see, when I believe that every word and every syllable of this book is God-breathed, when I look at the book, when I look at the passage and text, and when I look at the Word, I know *that* is the God-inspired Word the Lord has meant for me and for my people, as they listen to the exposition of the Holy Scriptures.

Just for example, take a sermon on Revelation 22:17. "The Spirit and the bride say, Come. And let him that heareth say, Come. And let him that is athirst come. And whosoever will, let him take the water of life freely." *Ha thelone,* "whosoever will." The Holy Spirit said to the Apostle John, Jesus' dear and sainted friend, "John, this is the last invitation in the Bible, and when you write that last appeal, don't write there, *'ha gnoskon':* 'whosoever understandeth,' let him come. Don't write there *'ha lamballon':* 'whosoever receiveth,' let him come. Don't write there, *'ha paskon':* 'whosoever feeleth,' let him come. Don't write there, *'ha philon':* 'whosoever loveth,' let him come. But, John, in this last invitation write, *'ha thelone':* 'whosoever will,' let him come. And I'll write his name in the Lamb's Book of Life, I'll wash his sins away. I'll save him forever. *Ha thelone."*

A sermon is an exegetical belief that every word is inspired of God. *"Ha thelone."* Then the message follows. I am not saved in my head, in my mind; I am not educated into the kingdom of God. Would it could be. Man, we'd just have schools and everybody would be saved and we could train them and educate them. I am not saved by the degrees or the education that I have, the more I may deny my image in sight of the Creator, as shown by the inhumanity of the highly educated Nazi Germans.

I am not saved in that I feel that I am saved. Feelings

can be graphed; if they are normal, they go up and down, up and down. Even love is a feeling. And if you tie your feelings to the gospel and your salvation, they'll drag you to death. One day you'll feel, "Oh, Lord, I'm saved, I can hear the angels sing, 'O glory to God.' " And the next day you are under the juniper tree, "Lord, Lord, I can't hear anybody pray; I'm lost. I was mistaken." No!

Then where is the seat of salvation? Right where God's Word said it was. *Ha thelone.* "Whosoever will, let him come." A man is saved by his will. He is saved in his volition. He is saved in a great decision that he makes. I cast my life now and forever with Jesus my Lord. I have decided to follow Jesus. That's where a man is saved. That's exegetical because I believe that every word in the Bible is inspired of God. In my preaching through the Bible I have found that if I follow the leadership of the Holy Spirit, I have a treasure and a knowledge beyond compare.

I announced to my people one time, "I'm going to preach through the life of Christ." And I took the *Harmony of the Four Gospels* and I started preaching through it. And then as the days and the months passed, I thought, "Dear God, it will be years before I come to the cross, and before I come to the empty tomb and the resurrection. Dear God!" Then it came to me, forcefully, why don't you do as the Holy Spirit says. The Holy Spirit took the life of Christ, told the story of the Lord, and came to the cross and the resurrection. Then the Holy Spirit took the life of our Lord, and the second time came to the cross and the resurrection. And then the third time he came to the cross and the resurrection. And then, as though that were not enough, a fourth time he followed the life of our Lord in a fourth Gospel, and for the fourth time came to the cross and the resurrection.

So I announced to the people the following Sunday

morning, "As of this minute we are going to follow the *Harmony* no longer. No longer. We are going to follow the Holy Word of God as the Lord inspired it in this blessed Book, and we are going to take Matthew and go to the cross. We are going to take Luke and go to the cross. And we are going to take Mark and go to the cross. And we are going to take John and go to the cross.

When I follow the inspiration of the wisdom of the Holy Spirit of God, I am following his mind and his order. And that's the most blessed thing that I could name, when a man stands in the pulpit to preach Jesus. Just as the Lord described in the Gospel of Luke, chapter 24, out of the Torah, out of the *Neveme* and out of the *Kethuveme,* he showed them all things concerning himself. And that's the way to preach. In that book, whether it is on this page, whether it is this one, whether it's this one, whether it's this one—all of it is God-breathed, inspired and inerrant; and it all points to Jesus.

Somebody came to Mr. Spurgeon and said, "Mr. Spurgeon, your sermons sound all alike." And he said, "That's right. Wherever in the Bible I take my text, I make a bee-line to the cross. That's the book. That's the Bible."

Second, preaching that the Bible is literally true. What does it do to the people? What does it do to my congregation?

Once, after I had been at our church for about a year, I announced to the people that I was going to preach through the Bible. I was going to start at Genesis and go to the last benedictory prayer in the Revelation. You never heard such lugubrious prognostications in your life. They'd never heard of anything like that. And the leading people of the church came to me and said, "Oh Pastor, oh-h-h, you will kill our church. It will burn. Nobody's going to come to hear somebody preach about

Habakkuk or Haggai or Nahum. I don't even know where they are." I grant you we had a problem. But it was a different kind than they thought. The problem was, "What in earth are we going to do with the people who are trying to crowd into this auditorium to hear the Word of the Lord."

And I went through the Bible for seventeen years and eight months. Where I left off Sunday morning, I began Sunday night. And did I hear people talking to one another! "When did you join the church?" "I joined in Isaiah. How about you?" "I joined in Galatians." "And you?" "I joined in 2 Timothy."

Right in front of our church is the YMCA, and the clerk over there said to me, "You know, the Sunday before a fellow came in here and said to me, 'I thought you told me that was a Baptist church on the other side of the street.' " The clerk said, "Well, it is. That's the First Baptist Church." "Well," he said, "it's not a Baptist church. It's an Episcopal church." And the clerk said, "What makes you think that?" "Well," he said, "I have just been standing on the steps watching those people as they come out after the benediction. And every one of them has a prayer book in his hand."

What happens when you preach that the Bible is literally true? People come to church with the Word of God in their hand. And they open it. We read it every service. We read it out loud together. And the deepening interest in what God has to say is unlimited. It is almost incredible, listening to what the Lord God has to say. It is a most astonishing and amazing development in this earth. You would think that the one who preaches the social gospel, when he stands up in the pulpit, has all the action. Man, he is with it. He's demonstrating and marching and rallying and he's out there in the forefront, leading social revolution and social reform. And you'd think, "Man, the whole world congregates around him to listen to what he has to say."

His church dies, he dies, the denomination dies, the institution dies. The whole thing dies.

And when I look at that and study it, it becomes apparent: when a man goes to church, he often hears a preacher in the pulpit rehash everything that he has read in the editorials, the newspapers, and the magazines. On the TV commentaries, he hears that same stuff over again, yawns, and goes out and plays golf on Sunday. When a man comes to church, actually what he is saying to you is this, "Preacher, I know what the TV commentator has to say; I hear him every day. I know what the editorial writer has to say; I read it every day. I know what the magazines have to say; I read them every week. Preacher, what I want to know is, does God have anything to say? If God has anything to say, tell us what it is."

And that's why the man comes to church. It's like King Zedekiah saying to the prophet Jeremiah, "Is there any word from the Lord?" Does God have anything to say? And Jeremiah cried, "There is." And that's our answer to the world today. "God has a Word. Hear ye the Word of the Lord. Thus saith the Lord."

I do not know of a better, finer descriptive sentence of what true worship ought to be than this one. In Acts 10:33: Cornelius, speaking to Simon Peter, says, "Now therefore are we all here present before God, to hear all things that are commanded thee of God." That's the purpose and that's the reason; and that's the best description of our worship services that I could ever read in any language in human literature. "Now are we all here gathered before God to hear all things that are commanded thee of the Lord."

"Preacher, do you have a word from God that will save our souls from hell? Do you? Preacher, do you have a word from God that will save our homes and our families from damnation? Do you? Do you have a word from the God that will save our children from the fire?

Do you? Do you have a word from the God that would deliver our nation from judgment? If there is a word, what is it, Preacher?" And when you deliver that message, that man will sit there and listen to you and he'll come back, and after thirty-five years he'll still be there, listening to the Word of the Lord.

What authority a man has when he preaches the infallible and true Word of God, as he stands on the immovable and everlasting Rock. You preach on politics and there may be half a dozen men out there who know more about it than you do. You preach on foreign affairs and maybe half a dozen men out there know more about it than you do. You preach on economics, or book reviews, or current events, or psychiatry or psychology, or whatever, and there will be somebody out there in the congregation who knows ten times as much about it as you do. But when I stand up and open my Bible and deliver the Word of God, you may know more about it than I do, but you're the only one.

I tell you, when I stand with that Book open in my hand, having prayed and prepared my message, I speak with authority. I stand on the Rock of the enduring ages. I am delivering the message of the Lord, and how different that is from a man who equivocates, whose unbelief is seen in the very gestures of his hands, tone of his voice, and the look on his face. You don't fool the people. If you don't believe, they immediately sense it and know it, and the equivocation destroys them.

I think of that fellow who didn't quite know, couldn't quite make up his mind. Reminds me of a fellow who swallowed an egg. He was afraid to bend, or it would break; afraid to sit still, or it would hatch.

When you preach the Word of God, one of the by-products, one of the corollaries, one of the addenda is what the world calls dogmatism. Dogmatics. There is a whole system of theology named that: "Dogmatics." This is the truth of God. We refuse to compromise it.

We refuse to attenuate it, extenuate it. We refuse to apologize for it. *This* is the Word of God. And the man who delivers it with authority and with conviction also has power. And the people are saved and God builds his church and the people are blessed.

Number three, what happens when I preach that the Word is literally true: I have spoken to what happens to me. I have spoken to what happens to my congregation. Last, may I speak to what happens to God. When I preach that the Bible is literally true, God is pleased.

Let us look at the beautiful story of the transfiguration. And the Father said this, "This is my beloved Son, in whom I am well pleased. Hear ye him." Let him speak. It's not my ideas. It isn't my persuasion. I haven't thought up the message. I'm just an echo, a voice crying in the wilderness. I just repeat what God has said and the Lord is pleased. When Satan, the most subtle beast of the field, began the destruction of the human family, that's the way he began. "Did God say? Why, don't you know these first eleven chapters of Genesis are mythological and legendary, don't you know that?" "Don't you know the story about the virgin birth comes out of fabulous fancy and mythology? Don't you know that? Don't you know that this thing of the resurrection of our Lord; don't you know that that was apparition and hallucination? Don't you know that?" That's Satan. And he destroys the preacher and his message. And with the preacher goes down the whole fabric and superstructure of the church of the living God. Tragedy, tragedy, tragedy. But when I believe the Word of God, the Lord is pleased.

You remember the fifteenth chapter of the book of Genesis, where old Abraham said to the Lord God, "You say one. My son out of my loins is to be my heir. And I won't have any son—just this servant Eleazar. I won't have any son. And I'm old and Sarah is old." And God took Abraham out under the chalice of the sky and said, "Look. If you can number the stars in the sky, you can number your seed that shall be born out of your loins."

And now the next verse. "And Abraham believed God and his faith was counted for righteousness." Abraham believed the Word and the promise of God and the Lord set it down; the Lord reckoned it on the side of righteousness. He's pleased when I preach that the Bible is literally true, that his Word is everlasting, yea and amen.

One other thing; when I preach that the Word of God is literally true, I place the Lord God under obligation to bless me. He is under oath and under promise to help me and to bless me. I put him under tribute and under obligation, when I preach his Word as infallible, inspired, inerrant, and true. One time a bunch of kids in our church, having some kind of to-do, put a big banner across the front. "If my people will . . . I will" (2 Chron. 7:14). "If my people will . . . I will." That's God. If I will, he will. And when I preach that the Bible is literally true, I place him under obligation to help me and to stand by me. He said, "My Word shall not return unto me void. It will accomplish that whereunto I have sent it." And when I preach the Word and deliver the Word of God, he is under obligation and duty and tribute to stand by me and help me and bless me. And he never fails.

Did you know they made a film of my life recently called, "This I Know." It's a film about this, my dedication to the Word of God. And in filming it they took me down about one hundred odd miles away from Dallas, to my first little rural church. And in the community the leading man in the church, after fifty-one years, is a boy that I won to Jesus. It came about like this:

There was a man in the community who was not saved. His wife was a Christian and he was not. I went to the home one evening and ate dinner with them, and after the dinner was over I sat down with that man and opened my Bible and showed him how to be saved. They had a son. And in order for me to be with the father alone, they sent the boy to bed. And when I talked to that father after midnight, he said, "No." And I went to bed so discouraged, so downhearted. I'd so prayed and asked God to bless me, and yet the man hadn't said yes to the Lord, wouldn't open his heart to Jesus. And I was so discouraged.

The following Sunday, down the aisle came that boy. Oh, he was about twelve years of age, and he said to me, "I have accepted Jesus as my Savior." And I said to him, "Spencer, you say you have accepted Jesus as your Savior. When did you do that?" He said, "Friday night. When you came out to our home and talked to my father. Do you remember, my mother and dad sent me to bed, sent me to my room." But he said, "I didn't close the door. I left the door open so I could hear what you said to my father. I listened to you until after midnight." And he said to me, "My father turned you down. But up there in my bed, I listened to what you said, and I accepted Jesus as my Savior."

No word ever spoken for God ever falls to the ground. Somehow, some way, in areas of life that we don't understand and don't know, God blesses it in his good purpose, in his elected choice, and in his heavenly time. That's the basis on which I have built, tried to build, with God's help the congregation that you call the First Baptist Church in the city of Dallas. We are right down in the middle of town. The shadow of a sixty-story building falls on us when the sun rises every morning. We are in the very heart of the city. By all odds and precedents the church should have died years ago.

What happened was this: When I went to the church, my predecessor, the eminent Dr. George Truett, had been there for forty-seven years. And when he died and they called me, I was forty-three years younger than the great pastor, Dr. Truett. The assignment was incomparably vast to me, and I got down on my knees and I said, "Dear Lord, if I preach this Bible faithfully, if I'm true to that Word, will you promise me that you will send me people from all over this city and build this church?" And I had the distinct feeling, still do, as deep as life itself, that the Lord God said to me, "You preach that Word and you be faithful to my Book and I will send you people. I'll raise them up and send them to you." That was thirty-five years ago. And in those thirty-five years I have never preached Sunday morning or Sunday night but that God has given us a harvest.

He has never failed. Not one time, however the floods, however the cold, however the odds, however the heat, however the holiday, however anything. There has never been a Sunday morning, never a Sunday night that I have preached in that church but God has given us a harvest.

Couples come to see me and they say, "We want you to show us the way of the Lord." And I say, "Who are you?" And they reply, "You never saw us before. You never heard of us. But we have heard you preach and we have come to seek the Lord." And then I tell them that is an answer to prayer. God said if I would be faithful, he would send us souls. And he has never failed. He doesn't ever fail or forget. His Word is like himself—the same yesterday, and today, and forever. May God bless us as we deliver that holy message of Jesus, undiluted, unadulterated, faithful, and true as the Spirit inspired its portrayal, its recording, its writing in this blessed Book.

R. C. SPROUL is president and staff theologian of the Ligonier Valley Study Center in western Pennsylvania. He is a visiting professor of Apologetics at Gordon Conwell Theological Seminary. Dr. Sproul holds a B.A. from Westminster College, a B.D. from Pittsburgh Theological Seminary, and a D.R.S. from the Free University of Amsterdam. He is the author of *The Symbol; The Psychology of Atheism; Discovering the Intimate Marriage; Knowing Scripture;* and *Objections Answered.*

HATH GOD SAID?
GENESIS 3:1
R. C. SPROUL

I think that we are all not only aware, but in many cases painfully aware, of the continued academic, technical, and intellectual difficulties that we face when we make an affirmation of the inerrancy of Holy Scripture. I trust that we have not been bathed in obscurantism to a degree that makes us ignorant of the avalanche of criticism that has been directed toward the church's classic position over the last two hundred years. And I hope that we recognize that much of that criticism may not be lightly dismissed. To do so, of course, would not be wise.

I think we are aware that it is our duty and the urgent need of the Christian community of our day, not to rest merely on the splendid statements of our fathers in defense of the authority of Scripture. Surely our generation is called to face the new issues that have been raised in academic circles. What I am saying simply is this: that there exist problems of an academic and intellectual nature with respect to the confessions that we are so bold to make. But that's not what I am concerned to focus our attention on this morning.

Bible quotations are from the *Revised Standard Version.*

For in addition to these questions of an intellectual nature, which at times indeed may be excruciating, there are other facets to this question that must never be overlooked. There is an emotional dimension. There is a psychological dimension. There is a theological, or perhaps what we may call a religious dimension that touches the heart of this issue.

As you recall a few months ago, I had the privilege in behalf of the International Council on Biblical Inerrancy to be involved in dialogue with a group of very respected theologians and biblical scholars in this country. It was a behind-closed-door session of question and discussion, clarification of our position, vis-a-vis theirs. The discussions went for an intense period of seven hours. And at no time during that discussion did it become one of vituperative or vitriolic exchange. It was a sanguine atmosphere and the discussion was carried on in the spirit of cordiality. But it was intensely academic in nature, and I believe that we were all weary at the end of it. What I recall was that after the discussions were over and we were moving to the parking lot, one of the elder statesmen of the other group who has been a friend and colleague of mine for years came up to me, not in a paternalistic way, but in a genuine fatherly gesture. He put his arm around me and said, "R. C., why do you get so exercised over this question? Why are you devoting so much of your time to the question of biblical inerrancy? Why can't we leave that aside and move on the real issues of reaching the fallen people of this generation?"

I'm sure that this man's primary concern was precisely that we get on with the business of the work of the church and of Christ and not be paralyzed by internal disputes and debates about matters like these. He was expressing genuine concern over my particular career as a teacher. And he was almost weeping as he raised that question.

As I stepped out of the academic and intellectual atmosphere that had characterized the previous hours and looked at him, I answered his question as emotionally as he asked it. And I said, "I can't help it. Scriptures are my life. I am not a second generation Christian. I came to Jesus Christ from the streets, and that's what brought me into the kingdom of God, the words from this Book. I love it. The contents, the message broke through the recalcitrance of my pagan heart and brought me into the kingdom of God and showed me the loveliness and sweetness of Christ."

And then in a statement of perhaps characteristic belligerence, I said to him, "No one will ever take this Book from me." And I had to admit candidly that I am somewhat prejudiced and emotionally involved in this question. I raised this point with him. "I understand," I said, "the difficulties that criticism has raised, and I know that many feel that as a matter of intellectual integrity they must set aside this doctrine, that they cannot cling to it merely for emotional or sentimental reasons. I must agree with the integrity of that." But I said to him, "What I would like to see when that happens, is that our Christian brothers and scholars who have abandoned this point lay it down with tears. And I haven't seen that."

I would think that if we came to the conclusion that this point of the faith of our fathers indicates an error of our tradition, and that we must abandon inerrancy, that if we did, in fact, come to that conclusion, that we would do it with tears, rather than in the attitude or spirit we have seen in some circles. I don't see this in evangelical circles, but in some circles there seems to be a certain delight and glee in finding difficulties in the text of Scripture. At that point it becomes religious, moral, and I think that we are facing the problem not only of the academic but the problem of enormous pressure to conform to contemporary drifts of opinion.

Many have said quite candidly, "It is not expedient for us to take such a stand in this day and age."

Again another candid and private conversation I had with a pastor for whom I have great respect and love. He said, "R. C., I am not a scholar. I am not an academician. I am not a trained and skilled apologist. I am a pastor and my concerns are pastoral in nature. Now, R. C., in my heart I believe in the inerrancy of Scripture, but I simply cannot defend it. I do not have the tools, the erudition necessary in this sophisticated era to make a good defense. And so I prefer not to stand for the doctrine." It was only a few months later that this pastor was asked in a public situation, "Do you, sir, affirm the inerrancy of Scripture?" and his response publicly was, "I do not."

Now it's possible that the man changed his mind in the intervening months between our private conversation and his public statement. But I am also recognizing the real possibility that the intimidation that he was experiencing was more than he could bear in his humanity. And who of us has not had to face that kind of pressure? Who of us has not succumbed to it at one point or another in our lives? We have sinned and do sin, my brothers and sisters, and we must be careful in this concern that we not give the idea that *we* are the ones who maintain a pristine purity of Christian life and obedience, while others have easily and quickly capitulated and negotiated the faith of Jesus Christ. We all have participated at one time or another in such capitulation.

We are often put to the test, and the test of our faith is very infrequently couched in terms of strict theological affirmation such as, "Do you believe *in God?"* We all confess that we believe in God, but the point at which we negotiate is a different question. "Do you *believe* God?" That's the issue. And that's where the point of testing is focused in our day. Now the idea of a test at the point of believing God is nothing new. And it's not an experience that we are facing as a first generation of the tested, but rather to God that *is* the test of fidelity.

Let me say it another way. The two greatest tests in the history of mankind focus the term of the test precisely on the point of whether or not the ones being tested believed God. I am referring, of course, to the test of our original parents in paradise and the test of our Redeemer in the wilderness. And I would like to direct your attention in the time that is remaining to an examination again of the terms and the circumstances and the outcome of those two critically important moments of test.

Let's look at the third chapter of Genesis. It begins with three words that appear to be innocuous in the text, but which the late E. J. Young throws into bold relief in his commentary as having interesting and significant import. Those three words are, "Now the serpent . . ." E. J. Young rhapsodizes on the significance of those three words as they introduce the third chapter of Genesis. Everything that has preceded those three words is a majestic statement of God's acts of creation. Everything is so positive and so lovely and so good and so true about God and his created order, until that note of dissonance is introduced into biblical history.

"Now the serpent . . ." It sort of suggests that something sinister and negative is about to be unfolded. And the words continue, "Now the serpent was more subtle that any of the other of the wild beasts of the field that God had created." This draws attention to the subtlety or craftiness of the creature being introduced. We read that this subtle serpent comes and speaks to the woman and asks what appears to be at the outset a harmless question, a request for information.

"Did God say, 'You shall not eat of any of the trees in the garden'?" The question again in the ancient version is, "Hath God said, 'You shall not eat of any of the trees in the garden'? " It's a very, very interesting question. You might wonder why the serpent raised the question in the first place. Was he just saying in "Columbo" fashion, "There's just one thing that I'm not quite sure about; do you mind if I ask you a personal question? Let's see if I have it right here. Did God say that you shall not eat of any of the trees of the garden? Is that what he said? Just wanted to get the record straight." Perhaps Adam and Eve were to assume that the serpent was doing a job of recording the facts for posterity.

I don't think that's what it was about here. But before I suggest what it was about, let me indicate another alternative. Do you think that the serpent did not know what God had said? Do you think that the serpent was ignorant of the terms of the probationary test that God had put before his creatures? I think the serpent knew very well what God had said. But listen to the subtlety of the question. "Hath God said, 'You shall not eat of any of the trees of the garden'? " What's the suggestion there? Satan knew very well that was not the case. They say, "No. In fact, God said we could eat freely of all the trees of the garden, but one. And that one, of course, he said if we touched, we would surely die."

Existentialist Jean Paul Sartre in the twentieth century has made it a matter of evangelistic zeal to maintain that unless man is utterly and completely autonomous, he is not, in fact, free. Sartre gives one of the most fascinating and clever arguments against the existence of God I have ever read. Traditionally we have argued, if there is man, and we have to explain and account for his creation, then there must be a God. Sartre turns that around; he says, "If man is, God cannot be. Because intrinsic to our notion of humanity is the concept of human subjectivity and freedom. And if there is a God to whom we are ultimately accountable and responsible, a God who has sovereignty over us, then we do not have autonomy. If we do not have autonomy, we do not have freedom. If we do not have freedom, we do not have subjectivity. If we do not have subjectivity, we do not have humanity." *Ergo.* "Since we do have these things, there is no God."

The point is very subtle; unless you are utterly and completely free you are not free at all, and Satan is raising that very point here. "Hath God said, 'You shall not eat of any of the trees of the garden'? " Every one of us has encountered this question of freedom in our own lives, particularly those of us who are parents. My daughter comes and asks, "Daddy, can I go to this rock concert in Pittsburgh on Friday night?" I say, "I'm sorry, honey, I have to say, 'No.' " And what do you suppose her response is? "You never let me do anything!" Put that one restriction there and the natural reaction is, "I'm not free at all." Unless I can have total freedom, absolute autonomy, I'm not really free; and that's the subtlety of the serpent that is being repeated again and again and again, even down to this very day.

But the test shifts from matters of subtlety to a direct contradiction and denial of what God in fact had said. Now the serpent leaves his "Columbo" methodology, becomes very straightforward, and says, "You shall not die, but you shall be as gods." I say that because so frequently I have heard it said that the initial slogan of humanism was the famous statement from Protagoras: *Homo neusura*—Man, the measure. Man is the measure of all things. No, my friends, the irony of history is that humanism's slogan does not begin with Protagoras; it begins with the serpent in Genesis who said, "You shall be as gods." An irony of ironies: the father of humanism was not even human.

Now it becomes a test of whom to believe. God says, "You'll die." The serpent says, "You will not die." Today some have said that's all right; they contradict but contradiction is the hallmark of truth. We say contradiction is the hallmark of the lie. Imagine the theory that contradiction is the hallmark of truth in this situation. Adam and Eve are wrestling with the dialectic. "God says, 'You will die,' whatever that means. This one says we will not die."

"Now that's a contradiction," says Adam. "And contradiction's a hallmark of truth, so this serpent must be the ambassador of the truth. And if God is the truth, then this must be God's ambassador who is now abrogating and setting aside the earlier prohibition. So let's go to the tree. It looks sweet; it's delightful; let's help ourselves." The issue in the Fall was the issue of believing God's Word.

Now let's go to the New Testament to the new Adam, and to the work that he performs immediately following his baptism. We read, "Jesus, full of the Holy Spirit, returned from the Jordan and was driven (or led) by the Spirit into the wilderness." Now, before we consider the content of the test of Jesus, let's take a moment to examine the scenario in terms of the differences between the temptation of the second Adam and the conditions under which the first Adam received his test.

The first Adam was subjected to a test of righteousness and obedience in the midst of a lush garden, a garden that provided for him all of the resources and benefits that he required to sustain his bodily needs. In fact, if I understand the test correctly, he was in a gourmet's paradise. Whatever he wanted to eat was there, readily available to him.

But the circumstance and the context of the test of Jesus was that of a fast. Not a three-day fast, but a forty-day fast during which Jesus ate nothing.

Jesus is not in paradise, but he was driven into the wilderness, outside the camp into the outer darkness into that desert place, which to be sure in one sense is the traditional meeting place between God and his people;

yet at the same time, it symbolizes that threatening, ominous state of fear and solitude. Solitude is quite significant for our consideration, because the test that is given to Adam and Eve is given to them in the context of a supportive community, indeed the most supportive community that God has ever instituted, namely that of marriage. When Adam underwent a test, he had at least the support of a helpmate that was suitable for him, who stood next to him, shoulder to shoulder. And as the evil one came to seduce them, to cause them to negotiate and compromise their loyalty and devotion to God, they had each other for mutual consolation and support. But Jesus was alone.

Again I take you back to the original account of creation where in every aspect of creation, after God does his work, he pronounces a benediction: "That's good." And yet the first malediction of biblical history comes when God sees something that is not good.

It is not good that man should be alone. God understands the anguish that is involved with one who is sentenced to solitude. Kierkegaard is eloquent on this point when he discusses the problem of existential solitude, pointing out that one of the worst punitive measures we can enact against a criminal is to place him in a situation of solitary confinement. Yes, indeed, there are moments when we crave our privacy, and even Jesus at times sought the respite of solitude, but how many of us could stand it for day after day after day? And then have to face temptation when we are alone.

But when we as Christians come together and sing together and work together, I feel a sense of encouragement welling up, a challenge to stand firm where I might, if left to myself, be quite willing to compromise my faith. And most of the sins of which we are most deeply ashamed are done in secret, things we would keep from the scrutiny and the knowledge of the community. There is a sense in which solitude gives us a certain freedom to do things that we might not do publicly.

This is not the sense in which Jesus is saying, "OK. I've just come out of the Jordan River and here publicly John the Baptist has sung the *Agnus Dei.* He has declared me to be the Lamb of God who taketh away the sins of the world. He said such marvelous things: that he is not worthy to untie my shoe laces. And now I'm being put to the test in front of the public." In that situation it would be difficult for Jesus to compromise. But now, it's off in the wilderness, by himself, no wife, no support system, utterly alone, no one there to offer restraints in terms of public opinion, and along comes that same serpent. And the point is not so much the contrast, but the similarity.

But . . . the issue is precisely the same. I have heard sermons on this many, many times, and I hear the text frequently read like this, "If you are the Son of God, *change these stones* into bread." The preacher focuses on the agony and anguish of Jesus' hunger, which, indeed, must have been great, but I think the point is in the beginning of this thing. *"If you are the Son of God,* change the stones into bread." Jesus is not confronted with the statement by Satan, "Jesus, since you are the Son of God, go ahead and change the stones into bread," or "Because you are the Son of God, go ahead and change the stones into bread." But he says, *"If* you are the Son of God."

Ah, there's that subtlety again. What were the last words, as far as we know from the biblical record, that Jesus had heard from the mouth of God? When he came up out of the Jordan River after his baptism, the heavens opened and the dove descended and a voice was heard saying, "This is my beloved Son." God had declared it. He had made an utterance to the effect that Jesus of Nazareth was his son. Now I suspect that if God, in this day, in this room, opened up the heavens and spoke to us directly and immediately, not through the medium of human authorship of the Scriptures or anything like that, but directly and immediately, and said, "This Book is the inerrant Word of God," the debates would be over.

But it wasn't over with Christ, because Satan came and said, "If you are the Son of God." I wonder. I don't want to be a heretic here and maybe wander to the rim of heresy to even ask the question, but I wonder if during that ordeal that Jesus suffered, the thought may have come into his mind, "If I am the Son of God, why am I going through this hunger? I am happy to do it, Lord, I'll hold out to the end, and I won't play with the stones; I won't eat; I won't break the fast. I'll do all those things, but this seems to be a very strange way for the Son of God to have to live." But that's the way Satan comes on. "*If* you are the Son of God." He is suddenly suggesting that maybe what God said at Jesus' baptism was not altogether true.

But Jesus responded quite differently from Adam and Eve. He said, "Satan, it is written." (I think it has been demonstrated once and for all that this has the force of a technical formula, by which the biblical authors are referring to sacred Scripture.) "It is written, 'Man shall not live by bread alone, but by every Word that proceedeth forth from the mouth of God.' Satan, the Bible says that I am not to live merely by bread. Now I am hungry. I would love to have a piece of bread. There is nothing I would like better than a piece of bread. But I don't live by bread alone, and you've forgotten that it is my duty to live by every word that proceeds from the mouth of God."

Our doctrine of inspiration confesses that the words of Scripture proceed ultimately from the mouth of God. We grant the mediation of human authorship and all the qualifications that are made, but we are speaking in terms of inspiration of the origin of this Word, as having been breathed out by God. And it is my duty, says the

Lord, to live by that Word. Now let's look at Luke's version of the temptation rather than Matthew's—the progression is different. (It's one of those problems we have to deal with.) "And the devil took him up, and showed him all the kingdoms of the world in a moment of time, and said to him, 'To you I will give all this authority and their glory; for it has been delivered to me, and I give it to whom I will. If you, then, will worship me, it shall all be yours' " (Luke 4:5–7).

The devil is saying: "I know the Father has promised you a blessing, if you go through your humiliation. You probably have some idea that exultation is at the end of the road, that all glory and power and dominion will be yours. But you have to go the *via dolorosa,* and this would make it so much easier, so much more expedient for you, since the end is the same. What difference does it make what means we use to get there? I can give you the same thing that God can give you: the kingdom. I can give you a kingdom here and all you have to do is genuflect ever so slightly. Bow one knee, that's all; we are out here in the wilderness and nobody's going to see you. John the Baptist will never know it. The multitudes who are to hear your sermon on the mount will have no report of it. Just one slight action of homage and it's yours."

And Jesus said, "That sounds so easy. But there's something you have overlooked. You'll have to excuse me, Satan, if I tend to be a bit rigid on this point, but it is written, *it is written.* You see, Satan, it says here, 'you shall worship the Lord your God and him only shall you serve.' "

And Satan says, "That's all right, you can still serve him. I'm not asking you to quit serving God; I am just asking you momentarily to give me a little homage. Why can't you serve us both? Oh, I guess I didn't read that text right, did I? 'Him only shall you serve.' "

"Satan, I can't serve two masters, and what you've

asked me to do is to choose this day whom I will serve, and the choice is clear. I go by what is written."

Satan responds, "But that was written so long ago. Is it really relevant to this live situation in which you are finding yourself today? Come on, certainly, Jesus, you have been a victim of the errors of your day and you are restricted by your human knowledge and living on the basis of *midrashic* tradition and the like; certainly we don't have to enforce that ancient prohibition that wasn't written by Moses in the first place."

Now very shortly Satan began to get the idea that this tack was not working, so his subtlety became even more intense. "And he took him to Jerusalem, and set him on the pinnacle of the temple" (v. 9). For you see, Satan perceived that Jesus was a very religious man. So he took him out of that isolated circumstance of the wilderness, out of the arena of profanity, and brought him into the temple's dominion itself. Indeed, to the pinnacle of the temple. It was comfortable, his Father's house. And then Satan says again, "If you are the Son of God, throw yourself down from here, for it is written . . . OK, Jesus, you have come after me all the time with this 'It-is-written' stuff, so let me give it back to you. I read the Bible too. I know what it says. Now look." Now it becomes a question of hermeneutics. "It is written," says Satan, " 'He will give his angels charge of you, to guard you,' and 'On their hands they will bear you up, lest you strike your foot against a stone' " (vv. 10, 11).

Jesus said, "I know what's in that Book. But does it not also say, 'You shall not tempt the Lord your God'? And, Satan, we must not set Scripture against Scripture."

What's Jesus saying here? He is saying that the Scripture prohibits us from putting God to a test of fidelity. "God has said as you have pointed out, Satan, that he will give his angels charge over me. Now at the present time I can look all around the temple and I can go back to the wilderness and look behind every bush, and I have to confess I haven't seen an angel in the whole forty days I have been here. I know that God says that he will give his angels charge, and I haven't seen any. So you want me really to see if God meant what he said. You want me to see if God's Word is trustworthy for this particular life situation I am in. You want me to jump off the temple and see if the angels catch me in their arms. Well, you see, there is something that you don't understand, Satan. What's going on here is not a test of God, but God is testing me."

Some have interpreted this text to suggest that Jesus is saying that Satan is inappropriate in testing Jesus, as touching his divine nature. And this is cryptically a confession of Jesus' deity by Jesus himself, saying, "You should not tempt the Lord your God, and since you are here tempting, or testing me, you are doing something that is quite diabolical which is your nature, namely: to suggest that I as the Lord God incarnate, may be tempted." I don't think that that is the point at all in the context. Remember that this test is being done to Christ as the second Adam. Jesus is representing man. I don't want to divide the two natures obviously, but I think that we can safely distinguish them at times, and here Jesus is saying, "I have no right touching my humanity, as one undergoing a test, as the second Adam, to turn that test around and throw it in God's lap. Why should God be put to the test? Has not the whole redemptive history demonstrated again and again that our God is a God of truth? Our God never violates his covenant. Our God never breaks his Word. The question of loyalty is not one that we can raise about God. The question that history raises is the loyalty of man. I am the one who is to be tested, not the Father. So go away, with your distorted applications of Scripture."

And we read that, "Satan departed from him until he could find a more opportune or convenient moment."

I want to conclude with one more contrast between them. Jesus believed God's Word indicating that he was the Son of God. Jesus believed God that angels would be given charge over him. Now we read in the Scriptures in Matthew's account that as soon as Satan departed, what happened? The angels appeared and embraced Jesus. They nourished his broken, mutilated physical body that had gone through this struggle and trial. I suggest that Jesus' physical appearance by the end of that forty days must have resembled that of a Mahatma Gandhi after a hunger strike. He must have experienced the ravages of the lack of food on his frame, and the angels came and embraced him and nourished him and applauded his triumph.

What happened when the tempter left the original Adam? There we read that the serpent left, and "God came back into the garden." Before, when our parents heard the voice, they walked in the cool of the evening. They were delighted and their souls were thrilled. They couldn't wait to go up and speak and have direct and intimate fellowship with God, but after their test, God came into their presence, and they fled and hid. They were naked; they were aware of their nakedness. They were ashamed. They were embarrassed to be in the presence of God because they had denied God.

Do you remember Peter standing outside of the judgment hall where his test came? Even after he had been warned as to what was at hand and prepared for it, when the test came, not by the princes of the church or the accrediting educational institutions . . . but some washerwoman came up and said, "Do you know the man?" not only did Peter say, "I don't know the man," but he began to swear he didn't know him.

And just as Jesus was being led from one of the places of judgment, as they were escorting him under arrest, the Scriptures tell us, "His eyes fell upon Peter." He didn't say anything. He just looked at him. That was the most painful moment of Peter's life, when he looked into the eyes of Christ, who even at that moment was going to deliver himself to the forces of hell rather than betray his Father. And Jesus looked at him and knew that Peter had failed the test.

"Do you believe God?" This must never be seen as a purely academic question. This is a matter that touches our faith in Jesus Christ. Faith, not in the sense of assent, but faith in the sense of fidelity. Do we live, or do we not live by every word that proceeds forth from the mouth of God?

I am weak, and you are weak. We are all too susceptible to subtle pressures and temptations to compromise on this point. But it is a real test. And it requires in our lives nothing less than a dependence on the grace of God from moment to moment and a clear recognition that we understand that our feet are of clay and that our frames are of dust and that we must cling tenaciously to that grace that God has given us. If left to ourselves, there would be no perseverance. And not only do we need the grace of God, but part of that grace and its outworking in this world is the support of the Christian brotherhood, the fellowship of the church, the communion of the saints. We are told again and again in Scripture, "Encourage one another." What we need in this hour is not simply knowledge and erudition, but I am convinced what we need is moral courage. And so I ask you to encourage me and to encourage each other and to encourage the church and even the world that God's Word is true.